VAMPIRES & VIOLETS

Lesbians in Film

ANDREA WEISS

PENGUIN BOOKS

To Greta

PENGUIN BOOKS
Published by the Penguin Group
Penguin Books USA Inc., 375 Hudson Street, New York, New York 10014, U.S.A.
Penguin Books Ltd, 27 Wrights Lane, London W8 5TZ, England
Penguin Books Australia Ltd, Ringwood, Victoria, Australia
Penguin Books Canada Ltd, 10 Alcorn Avenue, Toronto, Ontario, Canada M4V 3B2
Penguin Books (N.Z.) Ltd, 182–190 Wairau Road, Auckland 10, New Zealand

Penguin Books Ltd, Registered Offices:
Harmondsworth, Middlesex, England

First published in Great Britain
by Jonathan Cape Ltd., 1992
First published in the United States of America
in Penguin Books 1993

1 3 5 7 9 10 8 6 4 2

Copyright © Andrea Weiss, 1992
All rights reserved

Photograph credits appear on page 180.

LIBRARY OF CONGRESS CATALOGING IN PUBLICATION DATA
Vampires & violets: lesbians in film/Andrea Weiss.
p. cm.
Includes bibliographical references, filmography, and index.
ISBN 0 14 02.3100 5
1. Lesbianism in motion pictures.   I. Title.
II. Title: Vampires and violets.
PN1995.9.L48W45   1993
791.43'65206643—dc20   93-8634

Printed in the United States of America

Contents

Acknowledgments

This book would not have been possible without the help and encouragement of many people. The following friends, mentors, and colleagues read early drafts of one or more chapters and offered useful suggestions and criticisms: Christine Gledhill, Miriam Hansen, Dee Garrison, Judy Walkowitz, Trudi Abel, Jerma Jackson, and Su Friedrich. Michael Lumpkin of Frameline in San Francisco and Mark Finch of the British Film Institute each encouraged me to go public with my ideas by inviting me to present lectures on two chapters of this book. I am grateful to them, and to the many people who came to hear these lectures and ask questions or take issue with my work. These exchanges were an invaluable opportunity for me, providing crucial feedback and helping me to clarify my writing.

For enabling me to view the films, many of which are not in widespread distribution in New York and London (where most of this book was written), I would like to acknowledge the help of Sande Zeig during her tenure at First Run Features, Jan Rofekamp of Films Transit/Montreal, Patty White of Women Make Movies, Elaine Burrows at the British Film Institute National Film Archives, Charles Silver of the Museum of Modern Art Film Department, the staff of the Library of Congress – who accepted in their stride my requests for repeated viewings of *The Vampire Lovers* and *Lust for a Vampire* – and the many filmmakers who made their films and photographs available to me. For access to a wealth of archival materials, I am indebted to Roger Ritzmann of the New York State Censorship Archive, Joan Nestle of the Lesbian Herstory Archives in New York, the librarians of the Film and Theater Collection of the Lincoln Center Performing Arts Library and of the British Film Institute Library.

Acknowledgments

Much of this book was developed as part of my doctoral dissertation in the History Program of Rutger's University. I am fortunate to have had on my dissertation committee an exceptional group of people whom I respect immensely, both as scholars and as human beings: Jackson Lears, Harold Poor, Kate Stimpson, and Ginny Yans. My dissertation adviser and dear friend, the late Harold Poor, especially provided invaluable, enthusiastic, constructive criticism.

A more talented or more patient editor than Philippa Brewster I'm sure is not to be found. She had a persistent faith in me, and I am grateful for the privilege of working with her. I also want to thank Ulrike Ottinger, who offered me magnanimous support, trust and inspiration. And finally, a special word of appreciation and love goes to the late Vito Russo, author of the pioneering book, *The Celluloid Closet*. Vito was always generous with his vast film knowledge, his photograph and film collection, and his encouragement of my work. His far-reaching impact and creative influence on this earth will be felt for a long time.

This book is dedicated wholeheartedly to Greta Schiller, whose keen intelligence and unconditional love have made all the difference.

Introduction

THE COLOR VIOLET

'When you watch the film *Vertigo* [Hitchcock, 1958], are you Scottie [Jimmy Stewart] wanting Madeleine [Kim Novak], or are you Madeleine wanting Scottie to want you? Or both alternately and simultaneously? In what proportions and intensities?'

> – graffiti in the women's bathroom
> of the Lesbian and Gay Community
> Center, New York City, 1989

At the heart of this book lies a contradiction.
Lesbian images in the cinema have been and continue to be virtually invisible. Hollywood cinema, especially, needs to repress lesbianism in order to give free rein to its endless variations on heterosexual romance. Each lesbian image that has managed to surface – the lesbian vampire, the sadistic or neurotic repressed woman, the pre-Oedipal 'mother/daughter' lesbian relationship, the lesbian as sexual challenge or titillation to men – has helped determine the boundaries of possible representation, and has insured the invisibility of many other kinds of lesbian images.

And yet, this invisibility can foster visibility as well. Each instance of invisibility seems to leave a trace, if only a trace of its absence or repression, which is also a kind of image. These faint traces and coded signs are especially visible to lesbian spectators. Lesbians, moreover, have looked to the cinema, and specifically to these traces and signs, to create ways of being lesbian, to form and affirm their identity as individuals and as a group.

The contradictory relationship to visibility is captured in the meaning of the color violet, which has a long history of association with lesbianism. This association goes back to 600 BC, to the poetry of Sappho, who wrote of the violet tiaras she and her lovers wore in their hair. The fairy Puck,

I

in *A Midsummer Night's Dream*, gathers a magic purple flower to change sexual inclinations, and men and women in sixteenth-century England wore violets to indicate they had no intentions of marrying. As pansies came to signify love between men, violets (related to pansies in the Viola family) came to refer more directly to love between women. Earlier in our century, the lesbian poet Renée Vivien was called the Muse of the Violets, and Marlene Dietrich divulged that violets were a sign among Berlin lesbians in the 1920s. Alice Walker also knew the meaning of the purple flower, but her Hollywood producers clearly hadn't a clue what that was.[1]

The color ultraviolet, like most of lesbian history, is located just beyond the visible spectrum. Violet, as a sign of love between women, serves as an indicator of what lies beyond the visible spectrum and as a means by which to become visible to each other. It suggests a way for getting at the problem of actually finding lesbian visual images: to consider invisibility as well as visibility as a form of representation, and to look for signs that have different meanings for lesbians than they do for western culture at large.

The task of uncovering traces of a lesbian visual history is mindboggling, since not only is evidence of lesbian presence in the historical record negligible, but even evidence of its absence, erasure, or repression is elusive. A simple example of this is the problem I encountered while researching the photographs for this book. Regardless of how pronounced the lesbian dynamic is in a given film, the available photographs would feature a man and woman together in the frame. And regardless of the nature of the relationship between that male and female character in the film, the photograph would invariably suggest a heterosexual romance. Even the poster for the unabashedly lesbian feature, *Desert Hearts*, implicated a minor male character in the women's romance. Most available photographs are publicity stills, part of a publicity campaign appealing to and promoting heterosexual interests. Had I relied on film stills to locate films with lesbian characters and themes (rather than already knowing the films and therefore able to look further for photographs), I would have found nothing.

Patrice Petro, researching women's visual representation in another context, has found that what is required is not more evidence but a new approach to thinking about the past:

What is fundamentally at issue here, however, is not a lack of adequate documentation. In fact, because women have long been excluded from the texts and the documents of history, the process of feminist interpretation – of posing new relations between the visible and the invisible, the representable and the unrepresentable – necessarily entails a critical or transformed history and not a history predicated on the (illusory) fullness of empirical detail.[2]

This book looks at just this question of the relations between the visible and the invisible, the representable and the unrepresentable, while also eschewing the traditional historical approach of constructing an (again, illusory) progressive linear narrative of change over time. Instead its focus is on those periods in this century where the changes in the visual representation of lesbianism were the most significant, and on exploring the meanings behind these changes in representation for lesbian spectators.

There is a danger in using the term 'lesbian spectator', or even worse, 'lesbian identity', which assumes a coherent, unified position of identification among all lesbians despite wide cultural, racial, class and generational differences. Moreover, there is the danger of imposing the term on women who wouldn't have used it themselves. Many prominent feminists, for example settlement house pioneers Jane Addams and Mary Rozet Smith, or National Women's Party feminists Alma Lutz and Marguerite Smith, lived together in life-long relationships, continuing the concept of nineteenth-century romantic friendships well into the twentieth; they probably would have been horrified if the 'L' word, with its suggestion of deviance, were applied to them.[3] Even women who did acknowledge publicly the sexual component of their love for other women often defined themselves by other terms, as Jeanne Flash Gray did, recalling her life in Harlem in the 1930s and 40s, 'when we were Bull Daggers and Faggots and only whites were lesbians and homosexuals . . . '[4]

Throughout this book I try to draw distinctions between different ways of being lesbian, but ultimately I am forced to court these dangers, in part because I am ultimately more concerned with the private responses of a woman's heart and mind in the darkened theater than with how she defines herself socially or interacts with others. Of course this is a false distinction: her self-definition cannot be separated from how she views a film; her social visibility or invisibility influences how certain images of women are represented, and so on, ad infinitum. But lest this turn into a treatise on the impossibility of discussing anything at all, I am using the term 'lesbian' to refer to that aspect of identity which involves a woman's sexual desire for another woman, in all the myriad ways that desire is

3

named or unnamed, expressed or repressed, combined or conflicting with other aspects of identity.

The relationship of lesbians to the cinema has always been complex; it resembles a love-hate affair which involves anticipation, seduction, pleasure, disappointment, rage, and betrayal. For, until the last two decades, when some lesbian filmmakers began to produce films for lesbian audiences, the cinema did not intentionally address lesbian spectators. The few lesbian images offered by the cinema were created for heterosexual male viewers, to appeal to male voyeurism about lesbians and to articulate and soothe male sexual anxieties about female autonomy or independence from men. Still, lesbians did go to the movies, and did respond in different ways to these images. From the beginning, lesbians were able to subvert aspects of this powerful visual medium in order to create ways of being lesbian, to construct individual and group lesbian identities.

One means of subversion is the use of 'camp', a term that's hard to define and harder still to locate clearly within lesbian culture. Most definitions have focused on camp as an expression of gay male experience, and have excluded lesbian spectators from the privileged relationship between over-the-top female stars and their adoring gay male audiences.[5] But as a product of the closet and the pre-Stonewall bar culture, camp is a tradition which belongs to women as well as men, and existing theories of camp are in need of revision and feminization.

In the last few decades much more has changed in the cinema than the appearance of a few films which for the first time addressed, exclusively or inclusively, lesbian spectators. In fact, so much has changed that it is difficult to recapture the experience of going to the cinema in its golden years. The most powerful and popular cultural medium in the western world did not usually lower itself to resemble the everyday life of its viewers, but maintained its magical power by elevating its viewers to partake of its glamor. Mainstream cinema's decline in influence and quality over the last few decades has meant the loss of this glamor, on the screen as well as in the collective experience of going out to the grand old theaters. There is a final poignant irony here: just when the lesbian image (and spectator) is becoming visible, the cinematic experience has virtually disappeared.

I approach the subject of lesbians in the cinema both as a cultural historian and as an independent filmmaker. Yet neither identity is my underlying motivation for writing this book – which is, instead, simply my love for the movies. So often books about popular culture are written by theorists and intellectuals who exempt themselves from it; who as John Caughie has written 'can see the seduction but are not seduced.'[6] I have endeavored not to assign myself such a privileged position, but rather to write as someone who has deeply visceral, emotional responses to the cinema that may or may not resonate with those of other spectators. For this reason I tried to keep my discussions accessible to a wide, nonspecialized readership. Richard Dyer's insightful and enjoyable work on the cinema, especially his book *Heavenly Bodies*, has helped me to stay on this course.

As subjective and personal as my responses to films may seem at times, they are like everything else largely determined by historical and social experience. The difficulty, of course, is to avoid imposing my contemporary lesbian subjectivity on an investigation of the past. I don't believe this goal is truly possible for any historical inquiry, and it becomes doubly challenging given the dearth of historical evidence about lesbians. In order to stay within the realm of history and not cross into fantasy, I had to be content at times with simply raising the questions, realizing that some answers must remain beyond our grasp.

I

Female Pleasures and Perversions in the Silent and Early Sound Cinema

Lesbians and the cinema made their first appearance in the western world at the same historical moment. Of course, it may be argued, lesbians can be traced back to Sappho of ancient Greece, but the modern phenomenon of a woman whose identity (rather than merely behavior) is homosexual, only emerged in western Europe and the United States in the decades closing the nineteenth and opening the twentieth centuries.[1] The twin birth of modern lesbian identity and the motion picture in this *fin de siècle* era has meant that their subsequent developments have been irrevocably linked.

It is an odd claim, because so many other major social changes were also occurring in this period. Complex processes of industrialization, urbanization, the transformation to consumer-oriented society, all fundamentally altered people's perceptions of themselves and the world around them. So it seems misleading to single out these two social 'inventions' as having a special relationship. It seems odder still when one considers that lesbianism has rarely surfaced as subject matter in the cinema and that lesbians have never had even one female movie star to point to as an openly lesbian actress. Nonetheless, the cinema historically has played a major role in shaping the contours of lesbian desire and community. And conversely, lesbianism has had a major impact on the cinema (primarily through the threat it poses to patriarchal culture), influencing the way cinema represents women, represses and co-opts lesbianism, and is unrelentingly obsessed with heterosexual romance.

The idea that a woman's identity might involve sexual desire for another woman was greatly popularized at the turn of the century by the rather disturbing theories of a number of male 'experts' on female sexuality. British sexologist Havelock Ellis, in particular, scrutinized traditional women's friendships and labelled some of them socially dangerous and sexually perverted. Unlike his predecessor, the Austrian neurologist Krafft-Ebing, whose theories were based on women who rejected the feminine social role and exhibited male physiological traits, Ellis insisted that most lesbians were virtually indistinguishable from (although less attractive than) 'normal' women, and herein lay their danger. Not genetic anomalies or helpless victims (as Ellis sympathetically believed male homosexuals to be), the female homosexual, as man's sexual rival, was instead 'a woman on the make, sexually and racially dangerous'.[2]

To Havelock Ellis and many of his contemporaries it seemed that the lesbian population was increasing along with (and because of) the expansion of women's public roles in the turn of the century. As an acquired rather than congenital condition, female homosexuality was 'the result of the [female] college environments', unwholesome places which bred pathological attachments between women.[3] It was of course no coincidence that Ellis levelled his attack against the new women's colleges, not only all-female environments but ones which offered the possibility for intellectual growth, self-fulfillment, a career and financial autonomy from men. Ellis's position found support among American and British physicians and educators; medical journals reported that 'female boarding schools and colleges are the great breeding grounds of artificial [acquired] homosexuality'.[4] By 1910 in England and the United States, Ellis's ideas had moved from the pages of scientific tracts to those of literary and political journals, which began to use charges of lesbianism as a way of discrediting women's institutions and of launching a campaign against the New Woman.

The relationship between the history of ideas and their manifestation in popular culture is rarely (if ever) simple or direct. In this case, Ellis's preoccupation with all-female environments was taken up, popularized, and significantly refocused in several European and American films of the late 1920s and early 30s. Where Ellis saw danger, these films – especially two by female directors – imagined pleasure. *Mädchen in Uniform* (Leontine Sagan, Germany, 1931), *Club de Femmes* (Jacques Deval, France, 1936), and *The Wild Party* (Dorothy Arzner, United States, 1929) all focus on the joys rather than the perils of all-girl living; any potential danger is posed by an outside threat rather than by the women's attachments *per se*.

These films, set in women's schools, established a veritable genre that appears throughout movie history, continuing with the several remakes of *Mädchen in Uniform*, including a 1957 technicolor version with Romy

8

Schneider and Lily Palmer, and the Mexican version *Muchachas en Uniforme* (1950). Two films in this genre which retain *Mädchen in Uniform*'s female eroticism but abandon its radical feminist politic are *Olivia* (Jacqueline Audry, France, 1951), based on the autobiographical novel of English girls' boarding-school life by Dorothy Strachey Bussy, and *Theresa and Isabel* (Radley Metzger, France, 1968), the soft-core porn depiction of Catholic schoolgirl affection, featuring a memorable sex scene in the church pews. The lesbian vampire skin-flick, *Lust for a Vampire* (Jimmy Sangster, England, 1971), also exploits the setting of that hotbed of lesbian sexuality, the girls' boarding-school. Less sentimental, more vicious female relationships can be found in a somewhat different all-female environment also favored by the cinema: lesbianism is a prime 'horror' ingredient in women's prison movies, from *Caged* (John Cromwell, United States, 1950), to *Scrubbers* (Mai Zetterling, Sweden, 1983).

The classic, unparalleled girls' boarding-school film is the original *Mädchen in Uniform*. This early sound film was suppressed by the Nazis and virtually disappeared from film archives; the few prints to be found outside of Germany were assigned misleading or minimal subtitles that diffused the passion between the 'mädchen'. If remembered at all, it was only as an anti-Fascist film (which it also was) until feminists in the early and mid-1970s rediscovered it and established its significance as a lesbian film. Shown in a circuit of women's film festivals during the 1970s, it was once again, as it had been in the early 1930s, embraced by lesbian viewers who were thrilled to see such a strong proclamation of erotic desire between women.

Much critical writing has also focused on this film, of which B. Ruby Rich's article, 'From Repressive Tolerance to Erotic Liberation', gives the most in-depth analysis of the relationship between lesbian eroticism and political repression, and between the film itself and the circumstances surrounding its production. Rich places the film into the context of Germany's short-lived Weimar Republic, which witnessed a proliferation of gay and lesbian bars and journals, and flourishing movements for women's rights and homosexual emancipation. In 1928, when twenty-year-old American actress Louise Brooks came to Berlin to film *Pandora's Box*, she found, to her delight, 'The nightclub Eldorado [which] displayed an enticing line of homosexuals dressed as women [while] at the Maly, there was a choice of feminine or collar-and-tie lesbians'.[5] This subculture was familiar as well to *Mädchen*'s director Leontine Sagan, who was then a popular figure in Berlin's wild theater scene, and to the Berlin-based playwright Christa Winsloe on whose play the film was based and her lover, American journalist Dorothy Thompson.

While *Mädchen in Uniform* does take an anti-Fascist stance, the lesbian relations of the film are not merely a metaphor for the struggle against Fascism but are also, as Rich has argued, central to an understanding of this 'first truly radical lesbian film'.[6] The symbols of Fascism and patriarchy (the forbidding iron staircase, the sound of a bugle in the distance, the school principal whose function and image as 'phallic woman' embody these ideologies) are placed in juxtaposition with the unspoken, contained lesbian sexuality of the girls, which ultimately triumphs into full expression by the film's end.

As the prevalence of these symbols suggests, what is unusual about this boarding-school film is its militaristic, authoritarian, absolutely non-feminine atmosphere; it stands in for the girls' absent Prussian officer fathers, literally the absent patriarchy, rather than a loving female-defined space. The film's opening montage, as Rich points out, 'establishes an exterior world of military preparedness, steeples and archways, bugle calls, and the marching rhythm of soldiery'.[7] The symbolic forces of danger point to the world outside of the school, and not to the relationships between the girls within, as Havelock Ellis would have it. Erotic attachments between students develop in spite of rather than because of this environment. Instead, the school nurtures a particular relationship with erotic overtones between student and teacher; as Rich has insightfully described it, the adored teacher Fräulein von Bernburg (Dorothea Wieck) functions as an agent of repressive tolerance for such feelings: 'If the girls focus their sexual desires upon her, where the desires can never be realized, then the danger of such desires being refocused on each other (where they could be realized) is averted.'[8]

But this precarious balance is broken by a public speech by Manuela (Hertha Thiele), a young student who announces her love for Fräulein von Bernburg and precipitates a crisis that resolves favorably for her, von Bernburg, and all the schoolgirls. The school principal immediately recognizes Manuela's subversive action as a 'scandal'. As Rich explains,

> Despite the generally permissive setting, it is this act of pronouncement which constitutes the transgression of the school's most rigid social codes. It is the naming of what may well be known, this claiming of what is felt by speaking its name publicly that is expressly forbidden.[9]

The school principal was not the only one to find the spoken expression of lesbian desire scandalous. The American censors denied the film a license until certain cuts were made and subtitles deleted so as to obscure the passion between Manuela and Fräulein von Bernburg. While the theme of lesbianism persisted despite the mutilations, its political meaning was successfully defused. One change eliminated the line spoken by Fräulein von Bernburg in defense of Manuela: 'What you call sins, Principal, I call the great spirit of love, which has thousands of forms.' Film historian Vito Russo has written, 'This deletion, a political act, effectively removed any defense of such emotions and thereby perverted the intent of both [writer] Winsloe and [director] Sagan.'[10]

Although the censorship efforts in the United States would not go into full force until 1934, this early example of *Mädchen in Uniform* in 1931 set the tone for the next thirty years: lesbianism would be tolerated as subtext but any spoken pronouncement of desire, like Manuela's for Fräulein von Bernburg, was 'expressly forbidden'.

Despite (or perhaps assisted by) the changes inflicted on the film, it was an unmitigated success in the United States in the 1930s. Its appeal probably did not depend on its early, sophisticated use of sound or its innovative cinematic use of superimposition and montage, but on its reputation, no longer fully deserved, for treating a lesbian theme – which was becoming by 1930 the subject of public curiosity. According to the British film journal, *Close Up*, 'Even the large de-lux houses [in America], which have never before featured a foreign language film have played it and done splendidly with Frau Sagan's piece.'[11]

Most likely trying to cash in on the success of *Mädchen in Uniform*, a French male director, Jacques Deval, came up with *Club de Femmes* (English title, *The Girls' Club*) in 1936. In this film again, it is not the all-female environment which is dangerous but the male-dominated world surrounding and encroaching upon it. At the same time, however, this film is much more ambivalent about relations between women. The club, which is similar to a women's dormitory, is created as a haven of safety in the dangerous world of men; it is envisioned as 'a city, Femina, where no man may enter'. This female separatist environment is the realization of a dream shared by two middle-aged women, the director of the project and her 'friend', Dr. Aubrey, who becomes the house physician and whose sexuality is expressed through her tailored suits and her long looks at the female residents.

In the late 1920s and early 30s, one lesbian image appearing in popular fiction was that of 'the aging Lady in Lavender', as Carroll Smith-Rosenberg has described her. This sounds rather quaint and lovely at first, but the image was imbued with sinister intent. The aging Lady was found in all-female environments such as schools, settlement houses, and women's colleges; she was generationally-speaking the 'mother' to the New Woman, and played the role of her mentor rather than suitor. In this literature, she 'preyed upon the innocence of young girls, teaching them to fear men and their own sexual impulses'.[12] Previously confined to literary images, the aging Lady in Lavender moved into cinema through the characters of the women who run the Club de Femmes.

The film is divided into two primary plot-lines and several secondary ones. One of these is about a young woman who goes to great lengths to sneak her boyfriend into the residence, disguising him as her female cousin. The romantic scenes between this woman and her 'female' cousin are used for comedy; they ridicule both the situation of two 'women' in love and the idea that gender boundaries can be softened or crossed.

The other plot-line centers on the friendship of two women, Juliette (Josette Day), blonde, young, and innocent, and Alice (Else Argal), a brunette, slightly older, and more knowledgeable about the ways of the world. Alice is in love with Juliette, but fights the temptation to express it, so that her desire is visualized through tortured efforts at restraint. The exaggerated movement within the frame in those scenes where the two women are together works to convey this: Alice bends over Juliette as the younger woman is taking Alice's dictation, or holds Juliette to comfort her when she is upset, yet always freezes at a certain proximity, beyond which Alice will not move. The narrative also has Alice resisting Juliette: as Juliette wants to be closer to Alice (she has their rooms changed so they can be next door to one another), Alice, without explanation, draws farther away. And finally, the United States' Hays Office, enforcing the Motion Picture Production Code that had been put into effect two years earlier, also placed restraints on Alice's desire. *Club de Femmes* could only be released in the United States after some of the dialogue between the women was eliminated, such as a line in which Alice cryptically tells Juliette, 'You're so pretty . . . If I were a man, I'd really love you.'[13]

Finally Juliette is 'corrupted' by a man she believes is offering her a job, and Alice responds like a vengeful lover. She poisons the hotel's telephone operator, the woman who lured Juliette into the dangerous situation by playing on her innocence. Dr. Aubrey, immediately understanding Alice's motivation, calls her 'you unfortunate creature'. Rather than inform the authorities, the doctor sends her off to be a nurse at a leper colony as her punishment, at which point she is banished from the narrative.

In both of these stories, it is men who are dangerous, rather than the influence of women on each other as Havelock Ellis insisted. In the first story, the male intrusion into the female environment is initially portrayed as clever, harmless fun (while also discrediting the possibility of a true lesbian relationship) until the film passes its final verdict of disapproval when this fun results in unwed pregnancy. In the second, the man who corrupts Juliette is dangerous, while the lesbian who murders as a result is 'merely' tragic. Still, the film punishes the homosexual rather than the heterosexual transgression. It ridicules yet also substantiates the female separatist position of the club's directors, those aging Ladies in Lavender, while encouraging a sympathetic if somewhat patronizing view of those unfortunate female creatures who love women.

Vice Versa, the first lesbian journal in the United States (typed and mimeographed during stolen hours at work by a secretary who went by the anagram, Lisa Ben) ran a review of the film in 1947, calling the club 'a veritable Paradise for some who have no particular craving for masculine company'. It gave a detailed plot summary and concluded by highly recommending the film, despite the lesbian character's tragic ending,

> for all who enjoy reading *Vice Versa*, if only because the presence of a lesbian in the film is handled in a sane, intelligent manner rather than furnishing the usual subject for harmful propaganda or mere sensationalism.[14]

The following letter to the editor appeared in the next issue:

> I enjoyed your review of the Sapphilm, *Club de Femmes*. I saw it several times pre-war, but was not so sensitive to the lesbian innuendoes till I saw it revived recently. It made my blood boil when the lovely lesbian was exiled to the leper colony. XXX (anon.)[15]

This review and reader response indicate that at least some lesbians who saw the film found its treatment of Alice, but not her lesbianism, to be unfortunate or tragic; they rejected the negative cultural definitions of lesbianism. Of course, this letter also indicates the extent to which the social changes of the war years heightened lesbian perceptions; we have no way of knowing how lesbians who were 'sensitive to the lesbian innuendoes' when the film was first released responded to them.

There is no particular lesbian character, lovely or unfortunate, to be exiled in Dorothy Arzner's early sound film, *The Wild Party* (1929), only a lesbian subtext to a heterosexual romance which surfaces in particular scenes. Yet the film conveys a sensuality between the women and an unswerving devotion to each other which is absent from *Club de Femmes*. As Paramount's first sound film, *The Wild Party* retains the overly romantic, melodramatic qualities of silent film acting, which justifies an excessive female display of emotion, even when directed at other women. Dorothy Arzner was by far the most prominent woman director in Hollywood from the late 1920s to the 1940s, and also an overt lesbian. Male directors claimed to have tolerated her in the director's chair only because her lesbianism 'made her one of the boys' in the old boys' club which was Hollywood.[16]

Set in a women's college (modeled on Mt. Holyoke), *The Wild Party* displays the many pleasures of all-female living and the dangers of venturing outside of it, either to the local roadhouse, where drunk, aggressive men congregate, or to unchaperoned parties where men take advantage of women. Within the all-female dormitory, particular scenes – in which women dress provocatively as chorus line showgirls for a costume ball only attended by other women, or where Stella Ames (Clara Bow) jumps onto the lap of her roommate Helen (Shirley O'Hara) and embraces her – suggest a covert lesbianism that Arzner must have intended. This subtextual lesbian dynamic emerges later in the film, when Stella looks frantically for Helen and is disturbed to find her sitting with a man, George, by the seashore. George tries to reassure Stella that he loves Helen and would not take advantage of her, but he misunderstands the cause of Stella's alarm. She starts to cry and responds, 'I'm jealous, you see, I love Helen too!' In this shot Helen moves from George's to Stella's arms, and the camera moves to exile George from the frame while the two women romantically embrace.

Film historian William K. Everson has claimed that *The Wild Party*'s reputation for covert lesbianism was unfair; it revealed more about the spectator than the film. He wrote,

> If you're familiar with this 'manufactured' reputation for *The Wild Party* [and] are expecting a kind of 'Lesbiantics of 1929', you're in for a let-down. But otherwise, you'll find it a charming, refreshing and sprightly movie. It has amazing pep, vitality, and masculine gutsiness for a film directed by a woman, Dorothy Arzner, one of the few women . . . to make an impression as a director.

He ends his review by clarifying what spectators *should* be appreciating in the movie, according to gender:

> Women will love the fashions – which are tasteful and pleasing . . . and of course for the men, Clara [Bow], her wink, her sunny smile and her knees, are on generous display throughout.[17]

Mädchen in Uniform: The dangers of the girls' boarding school.

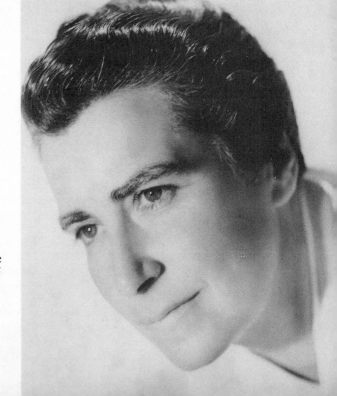

Dorothy Arzner: Considered "one of the boys" in the male bastion of Hollywood film directing.

Helen gazes lovingly at Stella, one of many tender moments between women in *The Wild Party*.

The Wild Party: Clara Bow's [second from left] "wink, her sunny smile and her knees" might be on display throughout the film for men, but this sexy chorus line show was staged for the all-female college audience.

Lesbianism in *Mädchen in Uniform*, *Club de Femmes*, and *The Wild Party* is conveyed primarily through the narratives and through the spatial relationships between the women within the frame. The characters are not visually coded as lesbians; rather, lesbianism takes the form of female identification. In key scenes in both *Mädchen* and *The Wild Party*, however, women are dressed in men's clothing: Manuela is in costume as Don Carlos for a school play when she makes her spoken declaration of love; Clara Bow wears a bowtie and suspenders when she sits on the lap of her roommate. These isolated crossdressing scenes in the context of a predominantly 'feminine' lesbian identification point to an inconsistency or confusion of visual codes. Historian George Chauncey has written that:

> The medical reconceptualization of female deviance as homosexual object choice rather than gender role inversion was underway by the 1920s, but it is difficult to date any such transition in popular images, in part because they remained so inconsistent.[18]

In these films, lesbianism pertained primarily to desire ('object choice'), but also surfaced as gender inversion. These images of crossdressing and gender inversion on the one hand (in the two key scenes mentioned above), and a feminine-identification involving a female object choice, on the other, were concurrent images in the cinema, and the former never entirely gave way to the latter.

During this same period, other films relied far more on crossdressing and other distinctive visual codes than on narrative function or spatial relationships between the women as a means of identifying lesbian characters or suggesting lesbian desire. These visual codes both drew from and further influenced styles that were important to the articulation of lesbian identity in the 1920s and 30s (see chapter two). In the 1910s, crossdressing and gender reversal were the basis for comedy in such films as *A Florida Enchantment* (Sidney Drew, U.S., 1914), where a female-to-male gender transformation serves as ironic commentary on male privilege but does not imply lesbian identity. By the late 1920s, however, some films had begun to use images of gender reversal to signify lesbianism, and to portray 'inversion' in a more serious light. The changes from the mid-1910s to the late 1920s in the meaning attached to similar images can be understood in the context of the popularization during this fifteen-year period of turn-of-the-century theories of sexual inversion.

One such theory was that homosexuals constituted a third or intermediate sex. In early twentieth-century western culture, a number of

17

sexologists as well as many homosexuals embraced this idea, although the latter rejected the pathologic implications of the former and called themselves Uranians, so named by British homosexual Edward Carpenter after the 'god of the nobler kind of love'.[19] British feminist Frances Wilder, for example, wrote to Carpenter, acknowledging that reading his work on 'the intermediate sex' helped her to realize her previously repressed sexual desire for women; she did not attach pathology to this sexual definition.[20] The 'intermediate sex' as a congenital condition was more frequently identified with male homosexuals, but it still influenced visual representations of lesbianism (both sympathetic and hostile), including the portrayal of a lesbian innkeeper in *Borderline* (Kenneth McPherson, U.K./Switzerland, 1930).

Borderline was an independently made silent film by a tiny English production company called the Pool group, which also published the English film journal *Close Up*.[21] In *Borderline* the Imagist poet H.D. (Hilda Doolittle) and her lover Bryher (Winifred Ellerman) star with Paul Robeson and his wife Eslanda in a complicated love triangle played out in a château resort in the Swiss Alps. The Pool group was particularly concerned with the workings of the unconscious mind, and this film was an experiment in how the unconscious might construct a narrative fiction. The underground style of the film relies heavily on montage and unusual camera angles to convey shifting subjectivities, and on light and shadows as metaphors for the film's racial themes. An anonymous pamphlet which accompanied the film, believed to have been written by H.D., points out how the characters are situated on or outside of psychological and racial borderlines.

Both H.D.'s and Bryher's characters are situated on a sexual borderline as well. H.D.'s unglamorized elegance suggests at times a feminized man, while Bryher, with her short hair and cigar, more consistently occupies an androgynous zone. Bryher's role as innkeeper of the resort places her strategically at the film's center, yet she is a marginal player who listens and observes rather than acts. By the late 1920s, according to Smith-Rosenberg, 'the concept of an "intermediate sex" [was used by Modernists] to symbolize an intermediate social role', and this is exactly the function of Bryher's character.[22] When she does take action, it is as an intermediary between polarized positions: first, to intervene against a white man who threatens Pete (Paul Robeson) in a racially motivated incident, and later, as the emissary of the town's white population which orders Pete to leave. In this later scene, her representation as a member of the 'intermediate sex' is transposed onto the racial conflict, and she serves as a bridge between white and black. After she has expressed her

Mädchen in Uniform: Manuela is dressed as Don Carlos when she makes her declaration of lesbian love.

The lesbian writer Bryher occupies an androgynous zone in *Borderline*.

sympathy to Pete, he repeats the phrase she has just spoken (or rather, the intertitles have given us): 'We're like that!' and for a moment the characters become linked through their marginality, their shared 'we'.

Richard Dyer has pointed out that whiteness (like heterosexuality) 'secures its dominance by seeming not to be anything in particular . . . '[23] It is only other racial and sexual identities which are defined, and these are so often defined by what they are not. In *Borderline* these racial and sexual identities remain marginal, but they are not in any sense lacking. In one scene where Thorne, a white man, comes to provoke Pete into a fight, Pete's greater moral force overwhelms Thorne's physical force, effectively turning the tables so that black is defining white by what it lacks.

Borderline was an underrated film which was poorly received in its day and which has never since received much recognition. Like the work of lesbian director Germaine Dulac, a pioneer of French avant garde film in the silent era, *Borderline* points to a long tradition of gay and lesbian filmmaking on the margins of cinema. Through its exploration of some aspects of German and Russian film styles of the Twenties, it created a disjunctive, experimental narrative. It also, rather subtly, subverted cultural assumptions about sexuality and race. Despite sexology's emphasis on pathology, *Borderline* suggests that the discourse on inversion was interpreted and utilized in more positive ways than sexologists had intended and historians have imagined. Although H.D. and Bryher had both personally gone to see Havelock Ellis over a decade earlier in order to make sense of their sexual orientation (Ellis claimed it was 'quite possible' that Bryher was a boy 'escaped into the wrong body'), *Borderline* identifies the 'intermediate sex' as a privileged social position. The Pool group was fascinated with the theories of Freud regarding dream analysis and the unconscious, but, by 1930 at least, seems to have been far more closely aligned with Edward Carpenter on matters of sexual inversion. The androgynous visual codes associated with Bryher's character further suggest that lesbians were able to use aspects of this 'medical' discourse in order to have a means by which they could become visible to each other.[24]

As all the films discussed in this chapter indicate, pseudo-scientific theories about lesbian sexuality were entering into public consciousness at this time, but they were not directly translated when given popular expression in the cinema. This is partly due to the strong female and lesbian influences in the production of these films, factors which point to the modification or transformation of sexologic theories within lesbian communities. *Mädchen in Uniform* and *The Wild Party* were informed by their directors' direct association with lesbian communities (in Berlin and Hollywood, respectively), while *Borderline* was strongly influenced by its nonprofessional lesbian actresses. Bryher's and H.D.'s creative input was not solely due to the film's marginal status, which allowed for a blurring of roles not possible in Hollywood, but was further strengthened by personal ties: Bryher was married to its director, Kenneth McPherson, in a convenient financial arrangement designed to deflect family attention away from her relationship with H.D. Given these lesbian interventions in the films' productions, it becomes clear that the forms of lesbian expression in the films were rooted in subcultural as well as medical models of lesbianism.

In the women's boarding-school and college films, the all-female environments became pleasurable rather than dangerous, with only hints of deviance attached to the lesbian character in *Club de Femmes* and with more positive associations of love between women in the other films. In *Borderline*, the 'intermediate sex' was linked to a privileged social position, suggesting that it gave the potential for resistance and subversion to the very people it was meant to control. Even the silent classic, *Die Büchse der Pandora*, or *Pandora's Box* (G.W. Pabst, Germany, 1928), the film of this period which most directly drew from the medical model of deviance (embodied in the character of Countess Geschwitz), offered images, through the vehicle of its star, Louise Brooks, which also contradicted and mitigated against this pathological model.

Havelock Ellis's belief that the female homosexual would recruit other women into 'the life' found its way, ironically, into *Pandora's Box* via the character of Countess Geschwitz. The irony here is that it was the less popular Sigmund Freud, and not Havelock Ellis, whose theories G.W. Pabst is best known for appropriating to cinema. Pabst's 1926 film, *Secrets of a Soul*, explicitly treated Freud's work on dream analysis (Pabst was subsequently a major influence on the Pool group in their production of *Borderline*). In *Pandora's Box* the influences of both Freud and Ellis are apparent, divided between the two female characters. The character of Lulu, played by Louise Brooks, is the embodiment of 'primitive', polymorphous sexuality which brings about the ruin of herself and everyone she comes near, while Countess Geschwitz, played by Alice Roberts, is a lesbian artist who takes a passionate interest in her. Lulu's innocence about her own sexuality and those around her makes her susceptible to, yet ambivalent toward, the Countess's overtures.

21

By the 1920s, a second particular lesbian image, other than the aging Lady in Lavender, had started to appear in popular fiction and sexual treatises as well as Modernist literature; with *Pandora's Box* it made its first move into the cinema. This portrayal has been characterized by Smith-Rosenberg as 'the aggressive seducer of other women, the ruthless, perverted competitor of the male suitor'.[25] Countess Geschwitz is probably the earliest celluloid lesbian of this model, visually and narratively coded as such through her costume (she's sharply dressed in a tweed suit and bowtie), through her romantic gaze at Lulu, which is competitively matched with that of a male suitor, and through the lengths to which she will go in order to save Lulu, including buying off blackmailers and succumbing to clearly distasteful heterosexual advances.

According to Louise Brooks's memoirs, Belgian actress Alice Roberts as Countess Geschwitz 'was prepared to go no further than repression in mannish suits'.[26] When she arrived on the set and was instructed to dance a seductive tango with Lulu, she responded with outrage. Pabst averted an emotional explosion by convincing her that she would be seducing him, not Louise Brooks: 'Both in two-shots and in her close-ups photographed over my shoulder, she cheated her look past me to Mr. Pabst, who was making love to her off camera. Out of the funny complexity of this design Mr. Pabst extracted his tense portrait of sterile lesbian passion . . . '[27]

Another result of this 'design' is that Countess Geschwitz directs her gaze in this scene not to Lulu but directly to the camera and thus to the spectator. One might therefore expect to find a lesbian dynamic emerging between the lesbian character and the female spectator. According to Vito Russo, this possibility was initially averted when British censors deleted the scene altogether and the expurgated version was used for the American film release as well.[28] But even with the scene restored, this dynamic is overshadowed by the performance of Louise Brooks as Lulu, who held a particular fascination for lesbian spectators. Brooks herself believed that her 'reputation' as a lesbian and her sexual appeal to both male and female spectators was an influencing factor in being chosen by Pabst to play the part of Lulu.[29]

Brooks was not a lesbian but rather, like Lulu, drifted around the edges of various sexual definitions. Her reputation for sexual ambiguity and gender transgression was nurtured both by rumor and by the various roles she played. In the same year as *Pandora's Box*, she played a handsome lad in William Wellman's *Beggars of Life*, and subsequently starred opposite German-Jewish dancer, silent film star and renowned lesbian, Valeska Gert, in Pabst's *Diary of a Lost Girl*, a film which dramatized highly

Pandora's Box: Countess Geschwitz is the cinema's first predatory lesbian. For Lulu's wedding, she's relinquished her tweeds but not her illicit desire.

French avant garde filmmaker Germaine Dulac: a pioneer of lesbian and gay filmmaking in the margins of cinema.

erotic tensions in a girls' reformatory. Brooks admitted to several affairs with women, including a brief one with Greta Garbo. But according to her close friend, the dancer Charles Weidman, 'Louise, everybody says you're a lesbian, but you're not really. You're a pansy.'[30]

Brooks proudly claimed that 'by the time I got to Hollywood, everyone thought I was a lesbian'.[31] She allowed the rumors to spread, to shock people and because she was truly attracted to women and to the upper class gay life. She traveled in fashionable lesbian circles, and her memoirs give us some insight into that famous yet closed world. While performing in the 1925 Ziegfield Follies, Brooks lived with her friend Peggy Fears, known for her affairs with all the Follies girls, and, according to Brooks, 'every man in New York was jealous of her conquests'.[32] Her other close friend was the notorious Pepi Lederer, niece of Marion Davies, whose girlfriend, Monica Morris, also ran around with Tallulah Bankhead. Bankhead's lesbianism was well-known because she wanted it to be so: she once told Louise Brooks that 'I only became a Lez because I needed the publicity – I had to get a job,' and went on, 'in the '20s and '30s, a Lesbian was tops in desirability, especially with a girlfriend as a side dish.'[33] Tallulah Bankhead, who was not cast in romantic roles and who couldn't have kept her sexuality a secret anyway, and Louise Brooks, who (like Clara Bow) was a casualty of the new Talkies, were women whose popularity rested in part on their value to shock. Their sexuality was only another item of curiosity, whereas for the carefully developed star images of Marlene Dietrich or Greta Garbo, public knowledge of their sexuality would have certainly meant the final curtain.

Much has been written about the impact of the cinema and particularly of such Hollywood stars as Louise Brooks and Clara Bow, Marlene Dietrich and Greta Garbo on the lives of young men and women in the decades of its ascendancy. Virtually all of this work has focused on the heterosexual values that the cinema instilled in young people, how the movies taught them to relate to the opposite sex, or whether the movies encouraged sexual behavior itself beyond the moral limits of respectable society. We know from sociological accounts of that time that the public's intense fascination with stars both provoked and answered deep desires, that stars served as a focus for excitement and sexual fantasy. A fashion critic in 1929 wrote,

> In recent years the popularity of the cinema and its far-reaching effects have made screen stars ... powerful in the determination of present-day fashions. The nationwide publicity which is given to

Louise Brooks in *Beggars of Life*: "Louise, everybody says you're a lesbian, but you're not really. You're a pansy."

them, has made them the popular heroes and heroines of the day. What they do, say, think, eat, or wear serves as a model for their devoted followers.[34]

What did this mean for lesbians coming of age in this period? How did they relate to the countless scenarios of heterosexual romance? How did they feel about the glamorous female star? The studies don't tell us this, but in reading between the lines it is possible to imagine. Certainly the intense popular appeal of the movies must have prevented some women from ever realizing that their fascination with the female star might be charged with erotic excitement, or that heterosexual romance could never quite be for them what it seemed to be for Douglas Fairbanks and Mary Pickford. For many of those who were conscious of their sexual attraction to women the heterosexual imperative of the movies must have prevented them from speaking of their private fantasies and longings. But although the cinema was, and is, fundamentally premised on the maintenance of the heterosexual order, it paradoxically also played a role in women's discovery of lesbian desire, and was borrowed from, drawn upon, reinterpreted and at times subverted by women in the process of constructing lesbian identity.

One sociological study of the impact of movies on teenagers in the 1930s provides ample testimony from young high school and college students on the lessons in gesture, movement, dress, and sexual technique that they gleaned from their favorite Hollywood stars.[35] This study, 'Movies and Conduct', was funded by a pro-censorship group, which raises problems in relying on it for historical accuracy. Still, the information is useful not only for what the young people say but also the way in which they say it. Unlike oral history interviews conducted many years later, these comments seem to provide genuine feelings and responses of people to the cinema at an early age. Although most of the accounts in 'Movies and Conduct' offer precise details of how information acquired in the cinema was put into practice in early heterosexual romances, a few stories revealing something about same-sex eroticism do get told. One sixteen-year-old high school sophomore confides, 'I've been thrilled and deeply stirred by love pictures and love scenes. Usually when I see them, it seems that I'm a looker-on and one of the lovers at the same time. I don't know how to describe it.'[36] These testimonies are generally explicit and detailed, down to the particular characteristics of particular male stars with whom the young women are in love. That this woman does not even mention which lover it is, male or female, she identifies with, seems a curious

26

evasion. Her inability to describe how she feels about the love scene and the lovers might be at the core of the problem for lesbian viewers who projected their own fantasies onto the scene.

Two other young women in this study, sixteen and seventeen years old respectively, put these heterosexual romances to work for them more consciously: 'I have one girlfriend that I love a good deal. She and I have been kissing each other "hello" and "goodby" [sic] for some time. It is on her that I make use of the different ways of kissing that I see in the movies.'[37] ' . . . I never wrote love letters but I practiced love scenes either with myself or [my] girlfriends. We sometimes think we could beat Greta Garbo, but I doubt it.'[38]

Sometimes the movies led women even further astray. One seventeen-year-old recounts how 'I always wanted to live with a girl chum. I saw many pictures where . . . girls roomed together. It showed all the fun they had. I decided I would, too. I ran away from home and lived with my girlfriend, but she was older than I and had different ideas, and of course she led me and led me in the wrong way.'[39] It is interesting that, out of all the movies which encourage heterosexual romance, this woman noticed instead the few in which two women lived together. Perhaps she is only able to tell this story by blaming her friend and by acknowledging that her behavior was 'wrong'. Certainly there are no accounts, out of the hundreds accumulated for the study, that indicate the movies positively encouraged a woman into lesbian self-awareness.

But does that mean it didn't happen? The evidence seems just beyond our grasp. The study indicates that the movies provided the stimulus for romantic fantasies which could often not be realized in the lives of the people interviewed, at least not at the age of sixteen or seventeen; that the movies led them to imagine experiences they were afraid or incapable of actually pursuing. The author of the study, Herbert Blumer, admits, in fact, that he found it improper and 'inexpedient' to print the full range of fantasies these young people derived from the movies, and he therefore selected only 'milder' examples to publish. He censored those more troubling fantasies which suggested behavior 'tabooed by the moral standards of community life'.[40] Those discarded stories might have held some answers.

Although movie stars wielded tremendous influence, for lesbian spectators the attraction to particular stars could not be a simple or direct relationship. In part this was because they were attracted not only to the image of the female star itself but to the way in which it could reject some of the feminine conventions imposed on it. Bryher gave some insight into this process of identification when she wrote in 1928 about her qualified attraction to Clara Bow (anticipating *The Wild Party* by one year): 'Dorothy Arzner should direct Clara Bow ... A film that brought across only her 'tough' amoral liveliness and cut out the beaded dresses and the sentiment would be a joy to watch.'[41]

Despite William Everson's instructions on where in the frame women and men should be focusing their eyes, women didn't always 'love the fashions' and there was nothing to prevent lesbians as well as men from enjoying Clara Bow's 'wink, her sunny smile and her knees'. But as Bryher's observation indicates, lesbians and heterosexual men (or heterosexual women) were not necessarily looking at or for the same things. The process of identification for lesbians was, and is, inevitably more complex, indirect, and selective than for heterosexual men who are cinema's intended audience.

Film theorist Jane Gaines points out that there are racial and sexual hierarchies of access to the female image. If, as she suggests, the white male look is the controlling gaze, while the black male look is repudiated or frustrated, lesbians cannot even be assigned a place in the hierarchy, since the lesbian gaze is illicit, taboo, and yet (secretly) readily available. Lesbians historically never have 'had the license to "look" openly', but at the same time illicit looking is what helped many lesbians realize their desire in the first place.[42]

So not only could lesbians selectively appropriate aspects of heterosexual film narratives or star images, but also the movies offered something special and particular to them. First, because the dominant culture offers lesbians so few images to identify themselves with, the rare surfacing of these images has had exaggerated importance and invariably has come to hold a special place within the lesbian subculture. Although such images are constructed within the contours of the dominant heterosexual culture and its reliance on models of pathology, the meanings attached to the images have been frequently transformed, either through women's involvement in production (as in the case of *Mädchen in Uniform*, *Borderline*, *The Wild Party*) or, more frequently, within the lesbian spectator's imagination.

But beyond specific images, the rise of the cinema and especially the Hollywood star system promoted the idea that different roles and styles could be adopted by spectators as well as by actors and actresses, and could signal changeable personalities, multiple identities. This new, twentieth-century theatrical sense of self was invaluable to the formation of lesbian identity. If not at the cinema, then certainly through the cinema, with its transformative powers and the allure of the theatrical, alchemical self, such fundamental twentieth-century lesbian experiences as 'passing for straight', crossdressing and masquerade, butch/femme role-playing, gay slang, and living double lives, were encouraged and legitimized. In other words, lesbians may have gone to the movies – like everyone else – to find romance and adventure, but they came home with much more.

'A Queer Feeling When I Look at You':
HOLLYWOOD STARS AND LESBIAN
SPECTATORSHIP IN THE 1930S

Boldly claiming to 'tell the facts and name the names', in July 1955 *Confidential* magazine embarked on telling 'the untold story of Marlene Dietrich'. The exposé reads, 'Dietrich going for dolls', and goes on to list among her many female lovers the 'blonde Amazon' Claire Waldoff, writer Mercedes de Acosta (rumored to be Greta Garbo's lover as well), a notorious Parisian lesbian named Frede, and multi-millionaire Jo Carstairs, whom *Confidential* magazine dubs a 'mannish maiden' and a 'baritone babe'.[1]

The scandal sheet may have shocked the general public by its disclosures, but for many lesbians it only confirmed what they had long suspected. Rumor and gossip constitute the unrecorded history of gay subculture. In the introduction to *Jump Cut*'s 1981 lesbian and film issue, the editors begin to redeem gossip's lowly status: 'If oral history is the history of those denied control of the printed record, then gossip is the history of those who cannot even speak in their own first-person voice.'[2] Patricia Meyer Spacks in her book *Gossip* pushes this definition further, seeing it not only as symptomatic of oppression but actually as a tool which empowers oppressed groups: '[Gossip] embodies an alternative discourse to that of public life, and a discourse potentially challenging to public assumptions; it provides language for an alternative culture.'[3] Spacks argues that through gossip those who are otherwise powerless can assign their own meanings and thereby assume some of the power of representation. Her concept of gossip as the reinterpreting of materials from the dominant culture into shared private values could also be a description of the process by which the gay subcultures of the United States

THE *Untold* STORY OF MARLENE DIETRICH

● Her very first success on the stage was singing a strange love song — from one girl to another. But her boy friends really flipped when she actually started living up the lyrics.

Famous men were chasing Marlene all over the world in 1936, when she met Frede, a slim, 20-year-old brunette. Their "friendship" was the talk of sophisticated Paris.

Confidential Magazine, 1955

A favourite hangout for Continental deviates is Carroll's, a Parisian club owned and operated by Frede. But few of the customers know that Dietrich helped to bankroll it.

Another baritone babe who's been linked with Marlene is the multi-million-airess Jo Carstairs, whose huge yacht took them on cozy weekends.

and western Europe in the early twentieth century began to take form.

Something that, through gossip, is commonplace knowledge within gay subculture is often completely unknown on the outside, and if not unknown, at least unspeakable. It is this insistence by the dominant culture on making homosexuality invisible and unspeakable that both requires and enables us to locate gay history in rumor, innuendo, fleeting gestures and coded language – signs that should be recognized as historical sources in considering the importance of the cinema, and certain star images in particular, to the formation of lesbian identity in the 1930s.

By the time her 'unspeakable' sexuality was spoken in *Confidential* magazine, Marlene Dietrich was no longer a major star. She had not yet stopped making movies, but she was not a major box office draw in the United States, and would soon return to the European cabaret stage on which she began. The appeal of her sophistication, her foreign accent and exotic, elusive manner, had been replaced by a new, very different kind of Hollywood star image, that of the 1950s all-American home-town girl, exemplified by Doris Day or Judy Holliday. Had the article been published in the 1930s when Dietrich was at her peak, it might well have cut short her career. The Hollywood studios went to great lengths to keep the star's image open to erotic contemplation by both men and women, not only requiring lesbian and gay male stars to remain in the closet for the sake of their careers, but also desperately creating the impression of heterosexual romance – as MGM did for Greta Garbo in the 1930s.[4]

But the public could be teased with the possibility of lesbianism, which provoked both curiosity and titillation. Hollywood marketed the suggestion of lesbianism, not because it intentionally sought to address lesbian audiences, but because it sought to address male voyeuristic interest. This use of innuendo, however, worked for a range of women spectators as well, enabling them to direct their erotic gaze at the female star without giving it a name, and in the safety of their private fantasy in a darkened theater. Dietrich's rumored lesbianism had been exploited in this way by Paramount's publicity slogan for the release of *Morocco* (Josef von Sternberg, 1930): 'Dietrich – the woman all women want to see.'[5] This unnaming served to promote intrigue while preventing scandal. Lesbians may well have suspected, for example, that Mercedes de Acosta and Salka Viertel were great loves in Greta Garbo's life, but the 'general public' only remembered that she once agreed to marry John Gilbert. (Garbo used to answer Gilbert's many proposals of marriage with 'ah, you don't want to marry one of the fellows'.)

What the public knew, or what the gay subculture knew, about these stars' 'real lives' cannot be separated from their star images. Whether these actresses were actually lesbian or bisexual is less relevant than how their star personae were perceived by lesbian audiences. This star persona was often ambiguous and paradoxical. Not only did the Hollywood star system create inconsistent images of femininity, but these images were further contradicted by the intervention of the actress herself into the process of star image production. Certain stars such as Katharine Hepburn, Marlene Dietrich and Greta Garbo often asserted gestures and movements in their films that were inconsistent with the narrative and even posed an ideological threat within it.

Marlene Dietrich's famous performance in *Morocco* is a case in point. During a cabaret scene, dressed in top hat and tails, she turns and suddenly kisses a woman on the lips. Vito Russo has written of this scene, 'Dietrich's intentions are clearly heterosexual; the brief hint of lesbianism she exhibits serves only to make her more exotic, to whet Gary Cooper's appetite for her and to further challenge his maleness.'[6] Dietrich biographer Homer Dickens also, though far less critically, viewed this scene in terms of its function to provide pleasure for men: 'the more masculinely she dressed, the more exciting [to men] her feminine appeal became.'[7] Certainly, such an androgynous image of woman – crossdressed, performing actions and assuming looks that traditionally belong to masculine domain – was appropriated by Hollywood and made less threatening by serving male fantasy.

In the scene, so shocking at the time, Amy Jolly (Marlene Dietrich) kisses the woman, then takes her flower and gives it to a man in the cabaret audience (Gary Cooper). This flirtation with a woman, only to give the flower to the man, is a flirtation with the lesbian spectator as well, by offering a potentially lesbian image only for the film to conclude heterosexually; as such her action in the scene is a microcosm of the film's entire narrative trajectory. But if we bring to the scene the rumor of Dietrich's sexuality, shared by many lesbians when the film was first released but denied to the general public (until *Confidential* so generously supplied it in the 1950s), we may read the image differently: this time as Dietrich momentarily stepping out of her role as *femme fatale* and 'acting out that rumored sexuality on the screen'.[8]

Not only rumor but also the scene's cinematic structure allowed lesbian spectators to reject the preferred reading (described by Vito Russo above) in favor of a more satisfying homoerotic interpretation. Amy Jolly's performance, in which she sings a French song in Dietrich's inimitable voice while making slow, suave movements across the stage,

Dietrich prepares for her sultry stage performance in *Morocco*.

Morocco: "Acting out that rumored sexuality on the screen."

is rendered in point of view shots intercut with reaction shots of the two contending male characters. Yet when her song is finished and she steps over the railing separating performer and audience, the image becomes a tableau. When Amy Jolly looks at the woman at the table, she quickly lowers her eyes to take in the entire body, to 'look her over'; she then turns away and hesitates before looking at the woman again. The sexual impulses are strong in this gesture, impulses that are not diffused or choked by point of view or audience cutaway shots. Dietrich's gaze remains intact.

Furthermore, in giving the flower to Tom Brown (Gary Cooper) at the close of the scene, she inverts the proper heterosexual order of seducer and seduced. Her costume, the tuxedo, is invested with power derived both from maleness and social class, a power which surpasses that of Tom Brown, who is dressed in the uniform of a poor French legionnaire. While he is 'fixed' in his class, she is momentarily able to transcend both class and gender. Such an escape from societal limitations can be seductive for all viewers, male and female; for lesbian viewers it was an invitation to read into the image their own desires for transcendence. Richard Dyer has pointed out,

> Audiences cannot make media images mean anything they want to, but they can select from the complexity of the image the meanings and feelings, the variations, inflections and contradictions, that work for them.[9]

This process of selection was especially important for lesbian spectators in the 1930s, who rarely saw their desire given expression on the screen. By providing larger than life cultural models, Hollywood stars exercised a captivating power over the public; for lesbian spectators struggling to define their sexual identities and with virtually no other models within the ambient culture, this power must have been intensely persuasive and attractive. Aspects of certain star images were appropriated by the growing number of women who began to participate in the emerging urban gay subculture, and played an influential role in defining the distinctive qualities of that subculture.

The early 1930s, of course, were the worst years of the Great Depression, and the emergent gay subculture in this period was largely metropolitan, middle class, and white. Antony James's claim in 'Remembering the Thirties' that 'it was a wonderful time to be in New York, to be young and to be gay' clearly didn't hold true for everyone.[10] But even individuals scraping by on shoestring budgets often saved for the Saturday matinee. And for those who could not afford the box office, the marquees, posters, and magazine covers made Hollywood stars into household images. Stars served as cultural models for a large spectrum of homosexuals across America, not only for those able to participate in the developing urban gay communities.

This fledgling gay subculture of the 1930s consisted of people who as yet lacked the self-consciousness to see themselves as belonging to a minority group. Unlike racial and ethnic minorities, they grew up in households where their parents not only didn't share their lifestyle but actively fought it with the help of the law, psychology, religion and sometimes violence. For a people striving toward self-knowledge, Hollywood stars became important models in the formation of gay identity.[11] The subtexts of films also provided the opportunity to see in certain gestures and movements an affirmation of lesbian experience – something that, however fleeting, was elsewhere rarely to be found, and certainly not in such a popular medium. This affirmation served to give greater validity to women's personal experience as a resource to be trusted and drawn upon in the process of creating a lesbian identity. Richard Dyer summarizes this process by claiming that 'gays have had a special relationship to the cinema', because of isolation and an intensified need to use the movies as escapism, because the need to 'pass for straight' elevated illusion to an art form, or because the silver screen was often the only place their dreams would ever be fulfilled.[12]

As Vito Russo points out in *The Celluloid Closet*, the film *Queen Christina* (Rouben Mamoulian, 1933) has in the past met some of these needs even though the lesbianism of the real-life Queen is not overtly depicted. He writes, 'In *Queen Christina*, Garbo tells Gilbert that "it is possible . . . to feel nostalgia for a place one has never seen." Similarly, the film *Queen Christina* created in gay people a nostalgia for something they had never seen onscreen.'[13] Greta Garbo herself complained that the Hollywood version of Christina was too glamorous and that Swedes who saw the film would expect a more realistic depiction. But despite Swedish audiences' expectations or Garbo's protests, her director, Mamoulian, insisted that Christina be glamorous and fall in love with a man.[14] Lesbian spectators, however, may well have appreciated the glamor even if they did mind the heterosexual romance. The lesbian poet H.D. certainly did; she expressed in words what many women must have felt:

> Greta Garbo, as I first saw her, gave me a clue, a new angle, and a new sensation of elation. This is beauty . . . Let us be thankful that she, momentarily at least, touched the screen with her purity and glamour.[15]

Garbo's stance and gestures in *Queen Christina* reinserted what Mamoulian, her director, tried to omit.

Although Garbo's glamor was unavoidable, she was able, through her performance, to undermine some of her director's intentions and compensate for what was omitted from the script. She brought to her portrayal of Christina sufficient sexual ambiguity for her movements, voice, and manner to become codes for lesbian spectators.

The scene in which Queen Christina kisses Countess Ebba on the lips expresses obvious sexuality, but there are other visual clues that allow for a lesbian reading. For example, the process of getting dressed in male attire seems to be a daily ritual for Queen Christina and her servant, their movements are so coordinated. Because of this the scene doesn't appear as a transvestite reversal, in which a woman transforms herself into a man, but rather that of a woman who remains a woman while rejecting the dominant codes of femininity, and the process is naturalized by the ease with which it is done. Within the same scene, Christina's story about Molière, who says that marriage is shocking, reverses the sentiment thus far spoken in the film that the Queen's not marrying is shocking. For viewers privy to the gossip about Garbo's relationship with the film's screenwriter, Salka Viertel, her inclusion of a quote from one of Molière's female characters, 'How is it possible to endure the idea of sleeping with a man in the room?' can easily be seen as a lesbian joke. Finally, the interaction between Queen Christina and Countess Ebba relies on the sexual innuendo of their dialogue and gesture, revealing the desire of the two women for each other and their frustration in having duty and responsibility interfere with that desire.

These double meanings are not completely accidental but were consciously brought to the film through Garbo's acting and Salka Viertel's writing. Salka Viertel had seen the film *Mädchen in Uniform* before writing the script for *Queen Christina*, and had known its director, Leontine Sagan, from her theater days in Berlin. Irving Thalberg, Viertel's producer at MGM, referred to *Mädchen in Uniform*'s lesbian theme when he asked her whether she intended 'Christina's affection for her lady-in-waiting [to] indicate something like that?' Thalberg didn't mind the association, perhaps because of the huge box office success of the latter, but also because he felt that 'if handled with taste it would give us very interesting scenes'. Through Garbo's and Viertel's connection to the upper class European lesbian community, subcultural meanings became embedded in a classic Hollywood film.[16]

In another key scene, the Chancellor tries to impress upon Christina the importance of marriage as a duty. When she responds 'I do not wish to marry, and they can't force me', there's a long silent take of her face, and she resumes with, 'The snow is like a wild sea. One can go out and be lost in it, and forget the world, and oneself.' This famous close-up on Garbo's face encourages the viewer to identify with the character's longing, as Andrew Britton pointed out, 'to make the spectator's experience of Garbo's face the analog of Christina's experience of the landscape'.[17] Her romantic choice of desire over duty could also have special resonance for lesbians who were struggling to make a similar choice in their own lives. When the Chancellor warns her that 'you cannot die an old maid', her response is ironic but with serious overtones: 'I have no intention to, Chancellor; I shall die a bachelor.' In this final statement she is no longer pleading to be understood, but has closed the debate by appropriating male language in the way she has appropriated male clothing to claim her power.

Such an act had a far different meaning in the 1930s than it would have today: appropriating male language or values was not male-identified or anti-feminist, but rather the opposite. Carroll Smith-Rosenberg, describing the New Women of the 1930s, writes, 'They wished to free themselves completely from the considerations of gender, to be autonomous and powerful individuals, to enter the world as if they were men. Hence they spoke with male metaphors and images.'[18] When viewed in this historical context, *Queen Christina* provides a strong lesbian subtext despite its director's attempts to purge the story from the taint of lesbianism.

Film theorist Mary Ann Doane defines the position assigned to the female spectator by the cinema as a 'certain over-presence of the image – she is the image'.[19] This female spectator position lacks sufficient distance from either voyeurism or fetishism, the two forms of looking on which visual pleasure is based, according to contemporary film theory. The notion of a feminine 'over-presence' draws on the Freudian argument that women do not go through the castration scenario which demands the construction of a distance between men and the female image. To simplify a complex argument, Doane finds that the theoretical female spectator's pleasure in the cinema can take the form of masochism in over-identification with the image, or of narcissism in becoming one's own object of desire, or it may be possible, by re-inserting the necessary distance, for the woman's gaze to master the image. This distance can be achieved through two kinds of transformation which Doane identifies as transvestism and masquerade. Female transvestism involves adopting the masculine spectatorial position; female masquerade involves an excess of femininity, the use of femininity as a mask, which simulates the distance necessary for the pleasure of looking.[20]

Lesbian desire seems to confound Doane's argument that women cannot assume the position of voyeur, or can only do so through temporarily putting on, like a suit of clothes, the sexuality of the male. In privileging the Oedipal complex, the psychoanalytic framework polarizes 'difference' along the lines of gender; it denies racial, class and sexual factors which play such significant roles in identity formation. Whether or not one accepts the psychoanalytic model, alone it cannot account for the different cultural positioning of lesbians at once outside of and negotiating within the dominant patriarchal modes of identification. Since the psychoanalytic approach can only see lesbian desire as a function of assuming a masculine heterosexual position, other, nonpsychoanalytic models of identification must be called upon, which can account for the distance that makes possible the pleasure the female image offers the lesbian spectator.

The Motion Picture Code of 1934 prohibited references to homosexuality in the cinema, resulting in a dearth of images that can be considered 'lesbian'. Since lesbian images have been chronically absent from the screen, even prior to the reign of the Code, it is questionable whether lesbians would enter into the spectatorial position of 'overpresence', of narcissistic or masochistic over-identification with either a virtually non-existent lesbian image or a pervasive heterosexual female one. When a star or her character can be considered lesbian, she is usually exoticized, made 'extraordinary' either by the star quality of the actress or by the power given to the character or, in the case of *Queen Christina*, both. In this way, the star system often served to distance lesbian spectators from the 'lesbian' star or character. Identification involves both conscious and unconscious processes and cannot be reduced to a psychoanalytic model that sees sexual desire only in terms of the binary opposition of heterosexual masculinity and femininity; instead it involves varying degrees of subjectivity and distance depending upon race, class, and sexual differences. For white working class lesbians in the 1930s, for example, across huge gulfs of experience, glamorous upper class white heterosexual star images often held tremendous appeal. For women of color, spectatorship was further confounded by the central role assigned to whiteness in standards of femininity and glamor, but it is possible that racial difference worked to create erotic fascination while also hindering identification with the star image. A black lesbian, recalling the movie stars that were important to her growing up in Chicago in the 1950s, looked back to films of the 1930s, especially *Morocco*:

Queen Christina has a private
moment with Countess Ebba, her
lady-in-waiting.

An April Fool's day issue of this
popular Berlin magazine advertised
Garbo and Dietrich as Siamese
Twins in a forthcoming film, *The
Tragedy of Love*.

I was just enthralled with Dietrich ... She has a sustaining quality
about her that I know has turned on thousands of women in this world.
I can't say I identified with her. I wasn't thinking in terms of black and
white in those days ... [It was just] lust, childhood lust, I'm sure.[21]

Although little evidence exists to fully clarify these questions, it is clear
that for a lesbian who perceived herself as 'butch', identification did not
require what film theorist Laura Mulvey has called a 'masculinization of
spectatorship' in order to connect with the male star, he who controls
the action and has a power that for two hours and 35 cents she could
appropriate. For a 'femme' the problem of spectatorship was also complex
and remains largely a matter of speculation.

An identification process thus complicated by different cultural and
psychosexual positioning places lesbians outside of conventional gender
definitions, as a gender inbetween, which partially explains lesbians'
attraction to certain androgynous qualities in the cinema. Lesbians who
were fascinated with *Morocco* and *Queen Christina* when these films were
first released spoke often of the allure of their 'ambiguity', a quality that
carries great appeal among people who are forced to live a secret life.[22]
In the 1940s, *Vice Versa*, the first lesbian publication in the United States,
recommended films to its readers based on whether they were 'fraught
with assuming innuendos and ambiguous significance'.[23]

The sexually ambiguous, androgynous qualities that Marlene Dietrich
and Greta Garbo embody found expression in the emerging gay subculture of the 1930s. Garbo and Dietrich were part of the aristocratic,
international lesbian set which was this subculture's most visible and
influential component; as such they played a role in defining the meaning
of androgyny for the small, underground communities of lesbians across
the country who saw their films and heard about them through rumor.
Writing about the use of androgyny in images by lesbian artists and writers of the period, Flavia Rando has observed, 'In an atmosphere heavy
with repressive theories, androgyny offered women struggling to create
a lesbian identity a possible alternative framework for self-definition.'[24]
Rando has found that for lesbians Romaine Brooks and Natalie Barney,
androgyny represented a spiritual transcendence of human limitations.
Katharine Hepburn's androgynous image in *Sylvia Scarlett* (George
Cukor, 1935) also offered this potential.

But while sexual androgyny was embraced as a liberating image by
some (especially more privileged) lesbians, it came to have a different,
less positive meaning within the dominant culture. Androgyny began to

be associated in the early twentieth century with the 'Mannish Lesbian', a concept developed by sexologists, particularly the Austrian Richard von Krafft-Ebing, as an expression of sexual and social deviance. As a new generation of women was moving out of the private sphere and into the public, transforming the traditional concepts of femininity, psychoanalysts and sexologists constructed the concept of the pervert, the invert, the out-cast, the 'Mannish Lesbian', as a boundary to restrict women's exploration of possible new roles. The 'Mannish Lesbian' was an image taken up by male sex reformers and modernist writers of the 1920s to symbolize social disorder and decay.

It is not, however, as though lesbians held one unified conception of androgyny while the dominant culture constructed an opposite, equally coherent one. Many lesbians in small towns across America had little access to the urban lesbian enclaves, and received whatever knowledge they had by reading medical journals (when they could get hold of them), often internalizing what little they could understand of their 'scientific' diagnoses.[25] And these diagnoses varied widely, from Krafft-Ebing's view of homosexuality as a functional sign of degeneration, to Freud's theories of childhood causality, to Havelock Ellis's distinction between 'sexual inversion' as an incurable congenital condition, and 'female homosexual-ity' as acquired and contagious. Katharine B. Davis's 1929 study, 'Factors in the Sex Life of Twenty-Two Hundred Women' reveals not only that homosexual relations were common (26%) among the unmarried women surveyed, but that by the 1920s, as same-sex relations were redefined as psychopathic, many women began to describe themselves as 'abnormal', 'unnatural', and 'pervers[e]', even though these terms were often at odds with how they actually felt about themselves.[26] Vern and Bonnie Bullough's study of twenty-five lesbian friends in Salt Lake City in the 1920s and 1930s shows that they discussed 'scientific' theories on homo-sexuality in order to understand themselves, yet consistently denied that they were 'perverts' or 'pathological cases'.[27] These studies suggest that while lesbians rejected much of the new sexologic theory, their partici-pation in the dominant culture insured that the 'Mannish Lesbian' and other models of deviance would have considerable influence on their self-images.

The historian Carroll Smith-Rosenberg has described the 'Mannish Lesbian' image as that of 'a sexually atavistic and ungovernable woman, associated with the 1920s bar culture and with European decadence'.[28] Dietrich and Garbo, certainly on some level, evoked this image of woman, Dietrich in her films and Garbo in the mystique that surrounded her personal life. Dietrich's image is virtually inseparable from the bar culture setting or from the decadent cabaret stage; even the film *Blonde Venus* (Josef von Sternberg 1932), a radical departure for her in that she plays a poor, devoted and selfless mother rather than an independent woman, has her performing some of her most outrageous cabaret acts to support her poor son.

Although as a cabaret singer in *Blonde Venus* Dietrich gives many performances, she appears in male attire – a white tuxedo – for the act only once: after she has been rejected by her husband and has had her son taken away from her. Because she has been portrayed as an unfit mother, and is now without husband or child, her status as an unnatural woman is confirmed by her crossdressing.

Garbo in *Queen Christina* and Dietrich in *Morocco* and *Blonde Venus* each evoke aspects of Smith-Rosenberg's description of the 'Mannish Lesbian' of the 1920s and 1930s as 'sexually powerful, yet ultimately defeated and impotent'.[29] Yet their androgynous qualities held a sexual appeal that the 'Mannish Lesbian' did not. They do function within the narrative as a sexual threat that must be contained; however, their appropriation of male clothing while retaining female identity, their aloof and inscrutable manners, and their aggressive independence provided an alternative model upon which lesbian spectators could draw. This model was an appealing departure both from heterosexual images of femininity and from the images of deviance that pervaded the medical texts.

Other films of the 1930s also used this double-edged image that at once subverted and confirmed the social order: the 1933 film *Blood Money* features Sandra Shaw in tuxedo with monocle, a contemporary lesbian fashion; in the 1934 British production *Girls will be Boys*, Dolly Haas momentarily and inexplicably transcends both of these gender categories when, in male drag, she sings and dances to a player-piano; Katharine Hepburn dons male attire and assumes the independence and privilege of men in both *Christopher Strong* (1933) and *Sylvia Scarlett* (1935); and the original German film, *Viktor/Viktoria* (1933) was closely followed by its British version, *First a Girl* (1935), both of which featured a woman who 'passed' as a homosexual man while projecting an image with lesbian over-tones. In the early 1930s, such recurring appearances of this crossdressing image were not mere coincidences, but embodied crucial debates that had begun to move from the pages of scientific journals and women's private diaries into public discourse. The Twenties had seen the publication of Radclyffe Hall's *The Well of Loneliness*, followed by censorship trials in the United States and England – which only insured that the novel's unmentionable subject matter would be mentioned in newspapers and at dinner tables across two continents. The lesbian-themed play *The Captive* created a sensation on Broadway. The debates over changing definitions of gender and sexuality in the early twentieth century were now fought out over the terrain of popular culture.

The cinema as the most widespread and powerful form of popular entertainment became an especially important battleground. The films addressed here are those that are stretched and pulled by struggles between images of powerlessness and power, between the dominant cinema's metaphor of sexual deviance and the inverting of this metaphor by female stars who brought to it a strong sexual appeal that the 'Mannish Lesbian' lacked, and by lesbian spectators who appropriated cinematic moments and read into them their own fantasies. Particular images generate meanings which are in conflict with their function within the narrative; poignant lesbian moments are constricted by the demands of a mandatory heterosexual resolution. The endings of both *Morocco* and *Queen Christina* can be viewed as affirming the heterosexual contract: they find their resolution in the feminization of the woman character, in the assertion of traditional gender categories and the triumph of the heterosexual order. But it is possible that lesbians also found pleasure in these resolutions, partly because the endings are relatively open, permitting a range of interpretations, and partly because the heterosexual relationships they promote are still considered unacceptable (for reasons of class and status); they are not the socially sanctioned relationships that the characters have been encouraged to choose.

In *Morocco*, even though Amy Jolly has been humiliated by Tom Brown (Gary Cooper), and has abandoned her independence and authority for him, she chooses to give up wealth and security for love. The unspoken eloquence with which she makes this choice and the extraordinary beauty of the scene evoke a sensation of pleasure in the film's resolution that for lesbian spectators may have made the heterosexuality and the powerlessness of Dietrich's character virtually irrelevant. In *Queen Christina* Garbo also renounces her 'bachelorhood', having fallen in love with a Spanish ambassador. She too relinquishes her power and status for love, a theme that could have resonance for gay male and lesbian spectators despite its heterosexual cast. In *Queen Christina*, the Spanish ambassador dies before they are united, leaving Christina alone to search for something that she hasn't yet known.

The endings of both *Morocco* and *Queen Christina* are, thus, complex and ambiguous. The romantic image of Amy Jolly following her man into the desert does not necessarily make for an affirmation of the heterosexual social order. Queen Christina's choice to relinquish the throne in order to marry the Spanish ambassador can be viewed more as an action to escape the narrow confines of her life of duty than as a heterosexual triumph. Amy Jolly and Queen Christina actually become more liminal and marginal in the films' conclusions, rejecting their past, their nationality, and their social position. Although each character can be viewed as having made the ultimate sacrifice in favor of a man, in doing so they've moved outside of the culture in which the heterosexual contract is constructed and maintained. In *Morocco*, Amy Jolly moves through the city's gate into the expanse of the desert, leaving her shoes behind in the sand, strong visual symbols for this departure from her culture. Queen Christina leaves on a ship, standing alone as its figurehead, her inscrutable Garbo face contradicting the aims of narrative closure. While heterosexual viewers might have found an affirmation of heterosexuality in the films' resolutions, lesbians could perceive the scenes as moving away from and rejecting the heterosexual social order.

Another example of how different historical spectators could have completely different readings is offered by the film *Sylvia Scarlett*, which endeared Katharine Hepburn to lesbians while it discredited her in the eyes of the general public. At its première in New York, the audience booed, yelled, and began walking out after twenty minutes; the New York *Sun* called it a 'tragic waste of time and screen talent'.[30] In *Sylvia Scarlett* Hepburn plays a girl who masquerades as a boy in order to help her criminal-father leave the country. But to the audience who has watched her transformation from 'Sylvia Snow' to 'Sylvester Scarlett', she's Katharine Hepburn in drag. In one scene a young male artist (played by Brian Aherne) looks at Sylvester Scarlett to make sense of his attraction to the young 'man', to understand why he gets 'a queer feeling when I look at you'. While gay men are the object of this mistaken identity joke, which acknowledges gay desire only as the expression of misinterpreted heterosexuality, lesbian spectators were able to select from the layers of Hepburn's star image – her rejection of female weakness as Sylvia Snow, her synthesis of masculine and feminine traits as Sylvester Scarlett – those gestures, expressions, costumes and looks which in the 1920s and 30s were being embraced by the emerging urban lesbian subculture as signs of lesbianism.

Sylvia Scarlett belongs to the generation of New Women that the sexologists had warned against. She takes on the stance of a man and has replaced her father's authority, temporarily at least, with her

46

Morocco: In the end, Dietrich follows her man.

Queen Christina

own. Yet Katharine Hepburn's image is not sexually threatening in the way that Marlene Dietrich's is in *Morocco* or Greta Garbo's is in *Queen Christina*. She does not try to appropriate male clothing, language, or manner as a woman, as 'Sylvia'; she only borrows from male prerogative when she attempts to pass as 'Sylvester', a boy. That the film is a comedy and she is presented as still a child further contribute to diffusing the danger she represents. Still, within the discourse of the dominant cinema she is a transgressor who is suggestive of the 'Mannish Lesbian': when her femaleness is detected, she will be called 'a freak of nature' and an 'oddity'. Such expressions reflect the new body of thought that shaped public consciousness in the early twentieth century, that saw homosexuality as deviance and the New Woman as sexual pariah.

But in *Sylvia Scarlett* certain qualities undermine this image of deviance, qualities that were brought to the film through Hepburn's performance, perhaps through director George Cukor's own homosexuality, and through the unique position of lesbian spectatorship. Sylvia Scarlett can be seen as outside of conventional gender definition, not as a man but as a different kind of woman. She represents the Trickster, a creative force that appears across time in literature and myth. Carroll Smith-Rosenberg defines the Trickster as being 'of indeterminate sex and changeable gender', and as 'a creature who exists to break taboos, violate categories, and defy structure'.[31] In *Sylvia Scarlett* it is the Trickster who suggests that her group should abandon crime and perform in a traveling carnival by the sea. The carnival world represents disorder and illusion, a twilight world closely associated with homosexuality, while the sea, as in *Queen Christina*, symbolizes the unknown, a place where identity is not already fixed.

In one crucial scene, Sylvia plays the wise fool; she speaks in riddles and tells disturbing truths. Her defense of another woman (played by Dennie Moore) reveals elements of femaleness, retained while in male masquerade – as the film's title, bringing together 'Sylvia Snow' and 'Sylvester Scarlett' into a third identity, confirms. Her crying out, 'I want the sea, I want the sea!' further suggests that she does not completely fit as either masculine or feminine. She momentarily steps out of the scene to address the audience directly, and here she turns the social order upside down (one of the Trickster's primary functions) by addressing, not the standard male viewer who is the intentional, omnipresent subject of most cinematic address, but women instead (as represented by the back of Dennie Moore's head in the lower left frame as a stand-in for the female spectator).

Katharine Hepburn on the set of *Sylvia Scarlett*.

But as Smith-Rosenberg has pointed out in her discussion of the Trickster in Virginia Woolf's *Orlando*:

> its inversion of order is transitory. It suggests but does not effect an alternative order. Woolf uses Orlando to expose the absurdity of rigid gender rules and the pomposity of the male literary canon. But Orlando changes neither England nor literature. She/he merely suggests what might be.[32]

Sadly, so too for Sylvia Scarlett. Her transcendence of human limitations is temporary, and the social order contains and remolds her behavior more than she can alter it. Similarly, the moments in *Queen Christina*, *Morocco*, or *Sylvia Scarlett* that have poignancy for lesbians are fleeting, transitory moments; they too simply suggest what might be and then are snatched from us by their incorporation into, and co-optation by, the discourse of the dominant cinema.

Film theorist E. Ann Kaplan has argued that 'to appropriate Hollywood images to ourselves, taking them out of the context of the total structure in which they appear, will not get us very far.'[33] We need to understand how the discourse of the dominant cinema works to contain the most threatening aspects of women's sexuality by using lesbianism as its boundary, to make what is unspeakable – in the case of *Sylvia Scarlett* – harmlessly laughable. Still, lesbian spectators have been able to appropriate cinematic moments which seem to offer resistance to the dominant patriarchal ideology, and to use these points of resistance and the shared language of gossip and rumor to, in some measure, define and empower themselves. As such, the cinema's contribution toward the formation of lesbian identity in the early twentieth century should not be underestimated.

In *The Celluloid Closet*, Vito Russo quotes the *Herald Tribune* review of *Queen Christina* when it first appeared: 'What do facts and theories matter? Christina, to all those who see Garbo's film, will always be the lovely girl who fell in love with the Spanish ambassador in the snow, and no amount of professional research will ever change her.'[34] For lesbian spectators who saw Garbo's film in the early 1930s, however, Queen Christina will always be the lovely girl who dressed in male attire and refused to marry, and no amount of heterosexual cover will ever change her.

3

Post-War Hollywood Lesbians: Whose Happy Ending?

I n the romantic comedy-thriller *Ghost* (Jerry Zucker, 1990), Whoopi Goldberg plays the role of a spiritual psychic named Oda Mae, who is an intermediary between Molly (Demi Moore) and her dead boyfriend Sam (Patrick Swayze). Toward the end of the film, she allows her body to be used as a medium so that they can touch each other one last time (Sam's spirit enters her body so that he can temporarily be made flesh). We see a close-up on her hands, a black woman's hands, wearing red nail polish, starting to take Demi Moore's white hands and caress them. But the close-up cuts to a medium shot showing their bodies moving toward each other, and in this cut Whoopi Goldberg has been replaced with Patrick Swayze. The scene continues as a romantic encounter between Molly and Sam, who no longer occupies the body of the psychic, but is now returned in his own (Patrick Swayze's) flesh.

We are asked to accept that Sam is a ghost, that he can walk through walls, jump on subways and have fights with live people, that he can talk or sing to a psychic and she can hear him, much to her regret. We are asked to suspend our disbelief and accept these things, and we do so readily because they are in keeping with the film's logic, with its very neat and consistent formulas. But asking us to accept a romantic incident between two women is perhaps asking too much. This scene is jarring because it is a false note, an awkward rejection of the guidelines the film has given us for how ghosts 'really' are and of its anything-is-possible premise. The madcap comedy quality of the film would seem to allow for the romance between Demi Moore (who looks like a 'dyke' throughout the film anyway) and her psychic, Whoopi Goldberg, while the dictates of the narrative would justify it, since the psychic's body is merely housing the soul of a white man. But the interracial, same-sex taboos prevent the scene from taking place, and the awkward signs of its repression become all too apparent.

For lesbians who go to the movies, even occasionally, it is no surprise that the primary forms of lesbian representation are, paradoxically, invisibility, erasure, repression. Strict censorship laws, and the many ways in which cinema addresses a heterosexual white male spectator, have conspired to maintain this invisibility. The lack of lesbian images, or of certain kinds of lesbian images, both within a film itself and through the history of the cinema, is therefore not a mere omission, but serves an important ideological function: that of monopolizing the representation of female sexuality with images of passivity and male dominance, images of being desired but not having desire. The absence or repression of lesbian images works to create and maintain the heterosexual 'sex/gender system' and the economic, social and political system it makes possible.[1]

Lesbianism in the dominant cinema has gone unspoken and often been visually excised, especially during the reign of censorship authorized by Hollywood's Motion Picture Production Code. Enforced by the Hays Office, the Code was on the books from 1934 to 1968, but reduced to a mere skeleton of its former self after 1961. It was instigated so that the cinema would not contribute to 'lower[ing] the moral standards' of the public, and to insure this, it stipulated that 'Law – divine, natural, or human – shall not be ridiculed, nor shall sympathy be created for its violation.' The Code did not specify whether lesbianism violated divine, natural, or human law, but it certainly was a violation, since the Code further spelled out that 'the sanctity of the institution of marriage and home shall be upheld' and that 'sexual perversion or any inference of it is forbidden'. With such guidelines, the Code made sure that American film scripts were altered. For example, the lesbian secret in Lillian Hellman's 1934 play, *The Children's Hour*, was replaced with heterosexual adultery in its screen adaptation, *These Three* (William Wyler, 1936). The joke going around Hollywood in 1936 was that, with the Code in effect, Samuel Goldwyn had bought the rights to an unfilmable play.[2] It did in fact remain unfilmable for another twenty-five years until Wyler could finally remake the picture, this time reinserting the lesbian plot and using the original title. And even then the film came up against the censors, in a confrontation which this time resulted in the regulations being considerably weakened. By the time *The Killing of Sister George* (Robert Aldrich, 1968) was produced, the censorship laws were giving way to the rating system, which assigned *Sister George* an X-rating. In some cities, however, the film was still banned altogether because, according to a Boston judge who banned it, its treatment of lesbianism was 'unsightly and lewd'. The Boston theater manager was jailed and fined, and in other cities an entire reel was deleted so that the film could be shown.

The Code, however, primarily concerned itself with direct references in the script, the elimination of which in no way insured against possible lesbian readings. Despite the Code's valiant attempts, lesbian desire could not be completely repressed, so that a lesbian dynamic can be perceived as the unspoken character motivation in, for example, *Johnny Guitar* (Nicholas Ray, 1954), *Old Acquaintances* (Vincent Sherman, 1943), *The Great Lie* (Edmund Goulding, 1941), and *Rebecca* (Alfred Hitchcock, 1940).

Hitchcock's *Rebecca* accomplishes a remarkable feat: it manages to convey both visually and narratively the sexual deviance of Rebecca de Winter while rendering her literally invisible. She never appears on screen because she has died before the story begins, yet her presence overwhelms the film, most strongly through the emotions she inspires in the other female characters: fear in the second Mrs. de Winter (Joan Fontaine), and obsessive desire in the sinister housekeeper, Mrs. Danvers (Judith Anderson). Mrs. Danvers's desire is expressed through the faraway, unfocused look in her eyes when she talks about Rebecca, although her severe look and harsh voice also, by accentuating her deviance, contribute to her being coded as lesbian.

In *Rebecca*, a young naive woman (the unnamed first person narrator played by Joan Fontaine) marries a wealthy widower, Maxim de Winter (Lawrence Olivier) and, when she moves into his mansion, discovers that the spirit of his former wife Rebecca still rules the household. The two wives are situated on opposite sides of the archetypal feminine virgin/whore dichotomy: the first wife is selfish, evil, and sexually uncontrollable (and punished accordingly), while the second is pure, selfless and nameless (and rewarded accordingly). It is only in rare moments of subtextual erotic fascination of the latter for the former that this sharp line seems to connect rather than divide the women. Although lesbianism is embodied in the characters of Rebecca's housekeeper and confidante, Mrs. Danvers (called 'Danny' by Rebecca), and the absent Rebecca herself, its diffusion throughout the plot means that it even extends at times to the character played by Joan Fontaine. The lesbian subtext originates in the novel on which the film was based – by lesbian author Daphne du Maurier – but film noir lighting styles and other cinematic processes contribute to casting a shadow of sexual deviance over the entire film.

In one scene set in Rebecca's bedroom, Mrs. Danvers looks intensely at the young, second Mrs. de Winter and tells her, speaking of Rebecca: 'She's too strong for you; you can't fight her. No one ever got the better

53

of her . . . Never, never. She was beaten in the end, but it wasn't a man, it wasn't a woman, it was the sea.' Mrs. Danvers then urges the Joan Fontaine character to drown herself – to join Rebecca in the metaphoric sea of sexual fluidity. An unstated erotic connection emerges in this scene between the first and second Mrs. de Winter, that of the ingenue fascinated with the (absent) sophisticated woman for whom Mrs. Danvers functions as intermediary. This dynamic, similar to that between Anne Baxter and Bette Davis in *All About Eve* (Joseph Mankiewicz, 1950), is further expressed in the masquerade ball scene in which the new Mrs. de Winter appears wearing Rebecca's costume.[3] Mrs. Danvers, who has engineered this fashion 'accident', is clearly the film's villain, while Rebecca is its obstacle to the heterosexual romance between Olivier and Fontaine. They thus perform the two primary functions of lesbian characters in Hollywood film noir.[4] By the film's conclusion, Mrs. de Winter's desire becomes refocused on the man, her husband, and Mrs. Danvers is destroyed by fire. One woman is cured and the other killed, foreshadowing the preferred approach to lesbianism in films of the Fifties and Sixties.

Richard Dyer has noted that film noir, a style popular in the 1940s and early 50s, provided an unprecedented number of homosexual images despite the stringency of the Motion Picture Code.[5] Although censorship records reveal an intense battle of wills between the Hays Office and film noir directors, the frequent recurrence of these images can be attributed to the way in which they were used to highlight psychological perversity as a dramatic ploy, something the Code might permit if it were adequately punished within the film's narrative.[6] In the case of *Rebecca*, censors insisted that Hitchcock sanitize Rebecca's character, writing that the film was in violation of the Code because of 'the quite inescapable inferences of sex perversion'.

They were particularly concerned about those scenes 'in which we get the quite definite suggestion that the first Mrs. de Winter [Rebecca] was a sex pervert'. For example, these lines by Mr. de Winter were considered offensive: 'She was incapable of love . . . She wasn't even normal!' and 'She . . . told me things I could never repeat to a living soul.' Hitchcock made a few minor changes but Rebecca's 'perversion' persisted nonetheless.[7]

In Hollywood films of the 1940s, 50s, and early 60s, lesbianism occasionally surfaces as a form of defiance in order that heterosexuality, such as the resolved relationship between Olivier and Fontaine in *Rebecca*, may appear the more natural and desirable. Whether remaining at the level of subtext or embodied in particular characters identifiable as lesbian, suggestions of lesbianism in the Hollywood cinema are encoded precisely in such ways as to encourage particular readings: as social deviance, sexual titillation/threat, and boundary against which 'normal' women's sexuality and social role are defined.

In the conservative social climate of the 50s and early 60s, the psychiatric literature renewed its fascination with the 'disease' of lesbianism. This fascination was partly a response to the burgeoning of gay subcultures in American port cities during the War years. War mobilization had taken men and women away from their families and small-town communities, and brought them into large, anonymous cities and same-sex military or home-front environments where they could more easily explore homosexual feelings.[8] The Kinsey Reports in 1948 and 1953 publicized and raised alarm about the unprecedented percentage of homosexuals to be found throughout the American population.

A study of lesbians in Buffalo, New York reveals that in the 1940s, lesbians began to meet and socialize in lesbian bars. By the 1950s, bars had become the center of an elaborate culture, with its own social rituals of dress and behavior, in which lesbians 'exchanged information about all aspects of their social lives, including sexuality'.[9] Although most lesbians continued to 'pass' as straight in the straight world, these considerable changes in lesbian self-recognition and identity meant that lesbianism increasingly revealed itself to the dominant culture. Not only did lesbians have to pass through the public space that stretched between their private homes and the bars they frequented, but membership in the subculture, especially for butch women, meant that their lesbianism became linked to certain visual and spoken codes which occasionally surfaced at work, in family gatherings, and in other aspects of the straight world.

Public concern about these disturbing developments which so flagrantly violated the strict heterosexual gender system of the Fifties was expressed through increasing stigmatization of lesbians under the guise of medical 'knowledge', which held a sacred place in the private life of middle America. A popularized Freudianism also influenced this medical model. Freud's case study, 'The Psychogenesis of a Case of Homosexuality in a Woman' (1920), located lesbian identity in women's rejection by their fathers, which in turn became transformed in the popular imagination to a rejection by or failure with men. A new generation of self-appointed experts such as Edmund Bergler and Irving Bieber wrote books trying to explain and cure homosexuality through psychiatry. Bergler fiercely believed that 'homosexuality – if treated appropriately, has an excellent prognosis and is curable in the short period of eight months in psychiatric-psychoanalytic treatment.' Throughout the 1950s and 60s, medical definitions of lesbians read something like this: 'sick, perverted, inverted, fixated, deviant, narcissistic, masochistic, and possibly biologically mutated, at best the daughter of hostile mothers and embarrassingly unassertive fathers'.[10] And yet, curable in eight months!

These definitions did not remain comfortably settled on the shelf in medical tomes but were taken up with grave concern by social scientists, popular writers, religious leaders, and others. J. Edgar Hoover warned against the lesbian 'twilight world' in an article in *American Magazine* in 1947, called 'How Safe is Your Daughter?' Paperback pulp novels with such giveaway titles as *The Twisted Ones* were appearing with frequency in the Fifties. Freud himself might even have excused such popular misinterpretations of his work, as he believed that 'perversion' could best be prevented by negative cultural views of homosexuality. He wrote that 'chief among these [preventative factors] is its authoritative prohibition by society . . . ' and in the absence of such prohibition, inversion would flourish.[11] Adherence to the (somewhat misinterpreted) medical definitions of lesbianism in these popular writings can be explained by the unimpeachable status of science, and particularly medicine, in the age of the experts; it is this status which, according to Sander Gilman, enables 'the conventions of medicine [to] infiltrate other seemingly closed iconographic systems'.[12]

One such iconographic system was the cinema. It was in this climate of increased gender conformity, and the simultaneous self-realization within the lesbian subculture, that walking clinical documents wandered onto film sets and into the public imagination. This medicalized homosexual image can be found in a range of movies from the period, from *Walk on the Wild Side* (1962) to *Seven Women* (1966) and most especially, in a film released in 1959 called *Children of Loneliness* or alternatively, *The Third Sex*, directed by Richard G. Kahn. This film, prints of which can no longer be found, actually uses an on-screen psychoanalyst (Wayne Lamont) who relates the case histories of his patients and warns against the dangers of 'abnormal sexuality'. The psychoanalyst subscribes both to Havelock Ellis's distinction between congenital inversion and acquired female homosexuality and to the post-war conviction that the latter variety could be cured through psychoanalysis. He tells Eleanor, a female patient (played by Luana Walters) who is troubled by her friend's affection, that 'What this girl offers to you is a false, barren substitute for the rich emotional life of a normal love . . . You should pity this girl. She undoubtedly belongs to that unfortunate class in whom this condition is congenital. She was born that way and there's nothing you or I can do for her. But you I can help.' In keeping with the formula of this era, one lesbian is killed, run over by a truck, and the other cured.[13]

Although the cinema fascinates with its ideological contradictions, its occupation of contested cultural terrain, it is difficult not to reduce these movies of the 1950s to agents of social control, so closely do they follow the medical model of deviance. According to sociologist Edwin Schur,

> Many current definitions of deviance and ways in which they are used function to keep women under control, or in their 'place', regardless of whether anyone has consciously intended that effect . . . We must then take into account the various ways in which men may gain, or think or feel that they do, as a result of the deviance labeling of women. Recent studies show that efforts at deviance-defining typically are grounded in the definers' perception that the 'deviants' pose some kind of threat to their specific interest or overall social position . . . There can be little doubt of the relevance of this notion to the situation of women. It is, indeed, axiomatic that male dominance depends upon female subordination.[14]

According to Schur's model for understanding deviance, lesbians are stigmatized for posing a threat, both to men's specific interest (by 'competing' for other women) and to men's overall social position. Since lesbianism suggests the possibility that women can be autonomous and independent from men, it is clearly the ultimate threat to male sexuality and to men's social, economic, and political dominance.

With so much at stake, how can we account for the changes in representation over the past twenty years, since the demise of the Motion Picture Production Code: the increased number of lesbian images that Hollywood has offered, or the relinquishing of this deviance model? Certainly they cannot be explained merely by the American Psychiatric Association's removing homosexuality from their list of psychiatric disorders in 1973. Some may see these changes in representation as deriving from a liberalization of sexual attitudes or as increased tolerance of lesbians, or as signs that the tyranny of heterosexuality is weakening. But to consider lesbian images since the demise of the Code reveals, on the contrary, the ways in which they still overwhelmingly serve heterosexual interests.

In the more 'liberal' films of the 1970s and 80s, the representation of lesbian characters has changed considerably yet they are still used to reinforce rather than challenge the heterosexual order. *Manhattan* (Woody Allen, 1979) offers a relatively 'positive' image of lesbianism in the character of Jill (Meryl Streep): she is attractive, confident, in a successful relationship, and does not come to a tragic end. Yet the fact that she has left Isaac (Woody Allen) for another woman is framed only through Isaac's perspective and is used to legitimize his paranoia and assorted neurosis. 'I think I took it rather well under the circumstances. I tried to run them both over with a car,' he explains to his soon-to-be new lover, Mary (Diane Keaton), and the joke works not only because of Woody Allen's wry delivery. Its success as humor depends on two cultural assumptions, one prevalent outside of the film text and one inscribed within it. The former is the cultural currency given to violence against lesbians: the belief that lesbians somehow deserve violence because implicit in their choice of women is a rejection of men, and that rejection warrants punishment. The latter is in the mode of cinematic address taken by the film, which assumes that the spectator is a man, and heterosexual, and will share in Isaac's feelings of victimization which would provoke a violent response. But this assumption does not completely preclude the possibility of a female spectator, in so far as the film also attempts to draw women into an identification with the male heterosexual spectator position.

The film uses a female character, Mary, to articulate these feelings of victimization ('That's incredible sexual humiliation; it's enough to turn you off women'). In this way the heterosexual woman embraces the masculine perspective on lesbianism as a rejection of men. That this comment is spoken by Mary also justifies the use of the second person pronoun, 'you', which speaks further to the male spectator and draws him into a sympathetic identification with Isaac. But since Mary also sees lesbianism from the position of the bruised male ego, the scene closes down the possibility for a female character to present any alternative perspectives while presenting instead this masculine position as a universal truth about lesbianism. Mary does briefly endorse the idea of two women raising a child together, but this endorsement is quickly squelched by Isaac's response, 'Really? Because actually I know very few people who have survived even one mother', and thus ends any alternative or feminist discourse.

The film makes abundantly clear, however, that despite sexual humiliation Isaac is still not 'turned off women'. His unrestrained heterosexuality and virile masculinity, despite appearances to the contrary, constitute a theme with which Woody Allen seems to be obsessed. Allen's use of humor exploits anti-semitic cultural myths in which Jewishness and masculinity are incongruous, and he rigorously asserts Jewish male sexuality as a corrective to the pervasive white Christian masculine ideal. He idealizes non-Jewish and desexualizes Jewish women characters, however, and this upholds rather than dismantles anti-semitic cultural myths about femininity and beauty.

The scene in which the character history of Isaac's ex-wife's lesbianism is revealed uses a tracking shot of a romantic getting-acquainted late night stroll between a man and woman who were known to be lovers in real life. The familiarity and 'normalcy' of this heterosexual romantic image provide the visual context for Jill's lesbianism and assure us that regardless of her claims (which she publishes in a book, further validating his paranoid fantasies), there is nothing 'wrong' with Isaac's sexuality. Lesbianism in *Manhattan* justifies the constant reaffirmation of a bruised but persevering masculinity.

When Jill's lover Connie hints that their son's drawing talents have been cultivated by her, Isaac responds, 'Yeah, but there's no way you can be the actual father.' This rejoinder relies on the kind of biological determinism often used to bolster heterosexual hegemony: procreative sex confirms the 'naturalness' of heterosexuality, which becomes the standard by which other behavior is judged and found inferior. The comment at once affirms the superiority of 'real men' by virtue of their sperm (in contrast with the lesbian lover's contribution of artistic skill), and places the lover, and with her the lesbian relationship, in a surrogate, 'unnatural' context.

Silkwood (Mike Nichols, 1983) also takes up some contradictory positions on lesbianism, and at times veils its promotion of patriarchal ideology behind politically progressive subject matter and a secondary focus on female friendship. The problem posed within this secondary plot is that Dolly (Cher) is in love with Karen (Meryl Streep), but Karen is not in love with Dolly. The lesbian character, therefore, is given desire but not the possibility for desire to be fulfilled. Richard Kwietniowsky has suggested a parallel between women's representation in heterosexual melodramas of the 1930s and 40s and in more recent Hollywood lesbian narratives: the lesbian character is crippled with homosexuality as a weakness, much as the 'wishing woman' of the Hollywood melodrama is crippled by her unrealizable desire.[15]

The frustration of this 'wishing woman' position is tangible in the scene of *Silkwood* where Dolly's love for Karen is made most explicit: she is sitting and crying, looking away from both the camera and the object of her desire when she says, 'I love you, Karen.' The spectator's gaze is positioned voyeuristically behind Karen as she enters the room, close to but not aligned with that of the heterosexual female character. The ensuing dialogue of 'I love you too', 'I don't mean I love you too', 'I know that's not what you mean, but it's what I mean', is constricted by both the inadequacy of language to express lesbian desire and the impossibility of its realization. The frustration of resorting to the same words to mean different things is further aggravated by the abrupt end of the scene when Drew (Kurt Russell), Karen's boyfriend, enters the room and asks, 'What's goin' on?', a question the spectator by now is most likely wondering as well.

As a contemporary liberal film, *Silkwood* allows its lesbian character to escape the fate shared by the 'wishing woman' of both the Hollywood heterosexual melodrama and the typical lesbian narrative, that of neurosis, alienation, estrangement, guilt or punishment. However, she is doomed to short-lived sexual pleasures with women who return to their husbands and to platonic intimacy with the woman she loves; in this regard she does recall Bette Davis's Charlotte Vail in *Now, Voyager*, who dares not ask for the moon but instead is grateful for the stars.

Dolly's unrealizable desire contributes to her role as an adolescent child mothered by her heterosexual friend. Karen's position as a mother is often established despite the fact that she is denied custody of her children; this incomplete equation of a mother without children lends itself readily to the adoption of Dolly as a surrogate child, which her name further implies. In the one sequence where Karen is shown with her children, Dolly accompanies Karen but like a modern adolescent daughter assumes no responsibility for the children (unlike Drew who does, with Karen's prompting). When Karen curses in front of her kids, Dolly teases, 'Don't say that, Mamma.'

Karen occasionally reprimands Dolly, but her maternal role more often takes the form of comforting her friend. Karen's problems at work should entitle her to some comfort as well, but Dolly doesn't reciprocate. At one point where both Karen's and Dolly's lovers have left them, the two women sit on the porch swing. One of Karen's hands holds a cigarette and the other is around Dolly's head, which rests on Karen's shoulder. Dolly cries and Karen comforts her, rocking the swing and singing a lullaby. The next shot, a side view of the house at night, lit inside to reveal the silhouetted movement of the two women on the porch swing, can be seen as a romantic image, but it is made safe by the mother/daughter framework that has been established in the previous shot, and by the continuation on the soundtrack of Dolly crying and Karen singing 'go to sleep you little baby', which undermines its romantic potential.

To a lesser extent, Dolly also takes up the role of child to Drew, or as the child within a reconstructed family in which Karen and Drew are the parents. When Drew comes back to Karen and the two are in bed together, Dolly runs into the room and climbs on Drew like an excited child whose father has just returned. Dolly is a welcome departure from most grotesque lesbian characterizations in Hollywood cinema, yet she reinforces the mythology of lesbianism as an adolescent phase while promoting the heterosexual nuclear family model.

The dialogue and action in *Silkwood* can often be interpreted as pro-lesbian, but these qualities are usually undercut by other cinematic processes. In the scene in which we are introduced to Dolly's lover Angela, Drew says, 'Well, personally I really don't see anything wrong with it', and Karen responds, 'Nope, neither do I.' This attitude of tolerance is expressed while Drew is facing the camera, cooking eggs on the stove, with Karen sitting at the table behind him. Since Dolly is their close friend whom they have long known to be a lesbian, the 'it' referred to here is not her lesbianism per se or any challenge to the social order that it might suggest, but merely the idea that she has sex with Angela. The liberal ideology of this scene emerges in both the role-reversal of Drew and Karen in the kitchen and in the reduction of lesbianism to a sexual act with no larger implications. The scene cuts to a shot of Drew and Karen driving up to the house, Drew at the wheel and Karen with groceries on her lap; already the 'proper' gender relations begin to reassert themselves. The spectator's gaze is then aligned with their point of view, and through the windshield we see Dolly and Angela moving Angela's belongings into the house. Karen and Drew's shock at this development is intended to be shared by the spectator, who, despite the spoken acceptance of homosexuality in the previous scene, is drawn into identification with the heterosexual point of view.

The liberal tolerance further retreats in a later scene in which Angela tells off Drew and walks out of the kitchen carrying her cosmetics tray (she's a beautician who works in a funeral parlor). Although she asserts herself verbally for the first time, the film tries to contain this assertion by aligning itself with the masculine position. The spectator's gaze is united with Drew's as he watches Angela exit the room, her naked legs and her ass (clearly outlined through her tight shorts) dominating the frame in a shot that suggests the common pornographic fantasy scene of the straight man conquering the lesbian. Shirtless and drinking beer, Drew becomes an image of generic masculinity, and then more rigorously so when the scene cuts to him outdoors, chopping wood. In a restoration of traditional gender representation, his masculine image is contrasted with Karen's sudden appearance in a short dress and high heels, for the first time in the film, as she asks Drew what she should wear and argues that 'honey, this [her clothing] is really important'. The short-lived role-reversal in the cooking scene has been replaced with an affirmation of masculine control and heterosexual norms once the lesbian character signals a threat through her aggression toward the male character.

Whatever their shortcomings, these examples of 'positive' (or at least not tragic) lesbian characters played by glamorous contemporary movie stars Cher in *Silkwood* and Meryl Streep in *Manhattan* might seem to indicate that the ugly old stereotypes of lesbians in the movies are a thing of the past. Caroline Sheldon, in her essay 'Lesbians and Film: Some Thoughts', has described these stereotypes as follows: 'the butch/mannish lesbian'; the 'sophisticated lesbian'; and the 'neurotic lesbian' (often 'femme' or closet).[16] Vito Russo, in *The Celluloid Closet*, thoroughly combs the history of Hollywood for lesbian and gay stereotypes, finding swishy queens, predatory schoolmistresses, sadistic gay Nazis, neurotic closet-cases, and more.[17] Russo's and Sheldon's findings are undeniably invaluable as a starting point for understanding how certain images of lesbians convey and reinforce negative associations. But the recent appearance of several attractive, 'unstereotyped' lesbian characters played by major female stars doesn't mean the dawn of a new, enlightened age of cinema; rather it points out the limitations of an approach to film criticism and spectatorship that focuses on and denounces gay or any other kinds of stereotype.

Richard Dyer has suggested that our thinking about homosexual representation must:

> go beyond simply dismissing stereotypes as wrong and distorted. Righteous dismissal does not make stereotypes go away, and tends to prevent us from understanding just what stereotypes are, how they function, ideologically and aesthetically, and why they are so resilient in the face of our rejection of them.

Dyer's work contributes significantly to such an understanding. He has begun by defining stereotyping as a process by which:

> the dominant groups apply their norms to subordinated groups, find the latter wanting, hence inadequate, inferior, sick or grotesque and hence reinforcing the dominant groups' own sense of the legitimacy for their domination.[18]

As both Dyer and Russo point out, gay stereotypes embody a wealth of hatred, fear, and disgust, and their far-reaching, detrimental effect on the lives of gay people can hardly be imagined. The anger with which gay people often react to Hollywood stereotypes is understandable and justified, but also raises new problems because this anger is often accompanied by and in fact based on an underlying, unspoken assumption: that non-stereotyped images are somehow more 'true', and stereotyped ones more 'false', as though somewhere there existed one ideologically correct image if only Hollywood would 'get it right'.

This application of a true or false test to the image suggests that it is sufficient simply to replace the stereotype with a more satisfactory image, without, as Simon Watney argues, 'fundamentally challenging or affecting the overall construction of gender roles – that which is taken to be "appropriate" to women and men – in film as a whole'.[19] It ignores larger problems of representation, by calling for the removal of the offending image but not questioning the ideological processes that gave rise to it in the first place.

The changes in Hollywood representation over the 1970s and 80s offer a test case which points out the inadequacy of such a simple substitution. Gay stereotypes obviously persist, but the past twenty years, coinciding with the unprecedented strength and visibility of the lesbian and gay movement, have witnessed their relative decline. In their stead we were offered a rash of what I have called the 'happen to be gay' syndrome, a form of representation new to films and television programs of the 1970s and 80s.[20] Here one finds a character who is supposed to be gay or lesbian in his or her choice of a sex partner, but looks and acts heterosexual in all other regards. If, as Richard Dyer has claimed, the use of gay stereotyping as a kind of visual shorthand explains the rest of a character's personality as being that of a gay person, 'happen to be gay' does the opposite: gayness explains nothing.[21] The character is just like anyone else; he or she fits the heterosexual model, and is visual 'proof' that there is no gay culture, identity, or history beyond the bedroom. In *Silkwood*, Karen and Drew never refer to Dolly's lesbianism but only to 'it', meaning sex with Angela. In attempting to eliminate the stereotype, Hollywood has also denied the cultural difference. In the process, 'happen to be gay' has become another form of invisibility.

Lesbian stereotypes, then, are not misrepresentations of reality that can simply be eliminated or corrected. Instead, they may be seen as indicators of ideological contradictions within a film between the promotion of dominant heterosexual values and the attempt to at once represent and repress lesbian desire. Annette Kuhn has proposed that although film narratives present a seamless, coherent world, and mystify the processes by which they do so, closer examination reveals contradictions straining to be reconciled. Kuhn has found that these sites of contradiction within a film are those moments that can most often lend themselves to alternative and feminist readings.[22] Stereotypes can signal such conflict by serving as absurd or grotesque reminders not to stray from 'normal' heterosexual behavior, while at the same time generating other, oppositional meanings.

The 'butch/mannish lesbian' stereotype, for example Beryl Reid in the title role of *The Killing of Sister George*, (Robert Aldrich, 1968), can lend itself to an alternative reading by holding within its own contradiction the potential to be seen as a transgressive image. Richard Dyer points out that as a stereotype, Sister George is defined by the norms of heterosexuality and therefore coded as 'masculine', but since she is not really a man she is 'therefore inadequate to the role ... Her straining after male postures is a source of humour.'[23] Her 'failure' as either a woman or a man, however, also offers the chance to view her inbetween status as the flagrant trespassing of gender boundaries.

George's 'failure' as a man will, through the course of the narrative, bring about her ruin, in the loss of her lover to another woman. This, according to Hollywood cinema, would not happen if she were a 'real' man. She is also ruined by losing her job – the character she plays in a soap opera is killed off when her motorbike, which she refers to as 50 cubic centimeters between her legs, collides with a more macho ten ton truck. George's 'failure' as a woman, on the other hand, offers her a measure of freedom. During the opening credit sequence, her lover, Childie (Susannah York), is confined within their home, wearing a scant pink outfit and visually coded as wife/child, while George is shown in a tweed suit, moving quickly and assertively through streets and alleyways. The negative associations that the dominant culture has attached to the 'butch' stereotype, which link Sister George's 'masculinity' to deviance, are not relinquished in this film, but they could be reworked in the minds of lesbian spectators in the 1960s, for whom 'butch' and 'femme' had a central place (and very different meaning) in the lesbian subculture. This highly eroticized and ritualistic role-playing was (and is) a way of organizing and acting out desire, and did not imply the deviance, either innate or acquired, that imbues the character of Sister George. Lesbians could project onto the 'butch' stereotype their own association with the butch role, even though the two meanings were incongruous. And despite Sister George's association with deviance, her rebellious spirit, including

A potentially romantic scene
between Meryl Streep and Cher in
Silkwood.

The clothes say it all . . . Beryl
Reid and Susannah York in *The
Killing of Sister George*.

her refusal to die in the filming of the soap opera accident scene, contradicts her victimization. According to Caroline Sheldon, some lesbian spectators were also able to appreciate 'George's outrageous anti-establishment behavior (particularly the incident with the nuns)'.[24] Although the film resorts to ridicule through stereotype and destruction through the demands of its narrative, Sister George cannot be fully subdued.

There are limits to this kind of oppositional reading, which is more readily available to some lesbians than to others. Audiences bring their own personal experiences and social histories to the viewing of films, and these obviously differ widely among lesbians. When the film was released, the censors were not the only ones displeased by it: the national lesbian organization, Daughters of Bilitis, also wanted it shut down, and urged lesbians to boycott it. The D.O.B. magazine, *The Ladder*, called it,

> . . . garish, noisy, [it] tinkles like tin cans in the trash, and purports to be a true picture of the lesbian underworld . . . *The Killing of Sister George* is an inevitable step in the progression of movies that appear to deal with lesbians, seen entirely through the eyes of heterosexual males . . .[25]

And the reviewer, Gene Damon (pseud. for Barbara Grier), finally concedes that 'there are some gay bar scenes that might be interesting to some people'. Evidence suggests, however, that the 'some people' who might be interested in the gay bar scenes far outnumbered the members of the predominantly white, middle-class Daughters of Bilitis, and that D.O.B., formed in 1955 to, among other goals, encourage lesbians to integrate better into society, was oddly out of step with the sentiment of many lesbians whose lives in the 1960s were centered in the lesbian bars.[26] Sister George's defiant and unsubduable behavior held more admirable qualities for those lesbians who did not share D.O.B.'s integrationist goals.

Lesbian images cannot be confined to one fixed or intrinsic meaning that spectators passively observe, nor has the dominant cinema been able to assimilate lesbian content on the level of narrative. As Richard Kwietniowsky has written, homosexuality 'cannot be accommodated within the normal structures of desire (principally the love story) because it is not prone to the same constraints or resolutions (such as monogamy, marriage, family)'.[27] His argument is stronger for those expressions of gay male desire which tend to depart more radically from these legally sanctioned social models, especially before the AIDS

66

epidemic necessitated so many changes in sexual behavior. Still it can be applied less conspicuously to lesbian desire, which cannot fit within the model for heterosexual romance either. Diane Hamer claims that:

> Given the difficult circumstances of lesbians' lives and the impossibility of fixing in law, through marriage, any lesbian love-affair, lesbian romance is committed to a less stable, yet ultimately more open-ended existence. Lesbian desire is renewable in a way that heterosexual desire is forbidden to be.[28]

Perhaps this is why the Hollywood film attempting to appropriate lesbian content also sets up questions that cannot be resolved by and within narrative closure. One example of this is *The Children's Hour* (William Wyler, 1961), in which the rumor of homosexuality and the scandal it creates finds its narrative solution in the punishment of the teachers through the downfall of their school. But despite this resolution, the question of the legitimacy of the charge of homosexuality remains an unanswered question that must be posed separately, requiring the second resolution of Martha's suicide.

Even this second attempt at closure cannot completely resolve the narrative dilemma posed by the introduction of lesbianism into the plot. It does successfully destroy the character of Martha (Shirley MacLaine) so that the lesbian potential between the two women can never be realized. But Audrey Hepburn's performance as Karen in these suicide scenes also provides an alternative reading – that the desire was mutual, shared by Karen as well, and therefore not totally destroyed by Martha's death. The film plot departs considerably from Lillian Hellman's 1934 play of the same name in this regard: in the play Martha shoots herself after she has confessed her desire and Karen dismissed it ('you never said it; we'll forget it by tomorrow'). In the film Karen responds to Martha's confession with a loving smile and suggests that they go away together to start their lives over – and then poor tormented Martha goes to her room and hangs herself. Karen's encouraging response to Martha's admission is one of a number of visual and spoken indications that Karen desires Martha as well. It is not that Karen is suddenly coded as 'lesbian', but something more dangerous. The ambiguous meaning of Karen's deep concern for Martha when she has locked herself in her room, or Karen's words in the final scene as she bends over Martha's coffin ('Goodbye, Martha. I'll love you until I die') suggest that the line between 'normal' and 'abnormal' desire is no longer so clear. Lesbian desire cannot be

different...

THE MIRISCH COMPANY PRESENTS

AUDREY HEPBURN
SHIRLEY MacLAINE
JAMES GARNER

THE CHILDREN'S HOUR

Because of the adult nature of its theme—this motion picture is not recommended for children.

With *The Children's Hour*, "tasteful" approaches to the subject of homosexuality were now permissible.

Martha (MacLaine) admits her love for Karen (Hepburn) in *The Children's Hour*.

isolated and confined to one tragic character, to be conveniently killed off.

Aspects of the plot work against such a reading: Karen fails to reach Martha in time, and has to resort to a phallic candlestick to break the door down, so suggesting the impotency of lesbian desire, while the *mise en scène* reinforces its perversity through the use of dark shadows and eerie music. Yet the possibility that Karen desires Martha emerges in these final scenes, resisting the film's desperate attempts at narrative closure. The varying interpretations of the film's final shot underscore this unresolved tension. Contemporary critics saw in the scene the reconciliation of Karen with her fiancé, Joe Cardin, when she walks away from the coffin and toward him in a last minute stretch for the classic 'happy ending'.[29] The feminist scholar Lillian Faderman claims that such an interpretation has 'nothing to do with what happened on the screen', and that there is no indication of a reconciliation in the film, as Hellman's play had originally suggested. Instead, Karen

> walks with her head held high, past the contrite townspeople who have come to the funeral, and past her former fiancé ... Her love for Martha and her tacit rejection of Cardin in this last scene hint distinctly at the possibility that Martha's confession has led Karen to her own self-realization which she is better equipped to handle than was Martha.[30]

Faderman's interpretation runs directly counter to that of the director's, but that does not mean it is any less valid. Wyler insisted not only that Karen is heterosexual, but that Martha is also 'innocent' of the charge of lesbianism, her admission notwithstanding. Wyler explained that:

> I wouldn't make a picture just about [lesbianism]. It simply wouldn't attract me. We're not out to make a dirty or sensational picture ... As I see it, it is a story that shows the effect of malicious gossip on *innocent* people [emphasis mine].[31]

When the Hays Office threatened to censor the film, Arthur Krim, then president of United Artists, backed up his director, guaranteeing that there would be no homosexuality, only a false charge by a malicious child.[32] Krim, by the way, threatened to proceed with the film without approval from the Hays Office, and suggested that if the Code regulations could not allow the film to be shown, the regulations, and not the film, should be changed. His threat paid off, and the Code, on October 3, 1961, was revised so that 'tasteful' treatments of homosexual themes were now permissible. Presumably suicide was what they meant by tasteful.

Martha Dobey is a remarkable screen lesbian, not only because she managed to get the Motion Picture Code changed, but also because at one point, just before her mandatory suicide, she does acknowledge her sexuality. She doesn't use the word 'lesbian' or 'homosexual' which could be a form of empowerment, through naming, and thus take her partially out of her role as a victim, but she does affirm what others have accused her of: she loved Karen 'that way . . . the way they said I loved you'. More frequently, the lesbian character has been burdened with an additional problem in that her sexuality is not named, and certainly not by herself. Rather, in pre-1970 Hollywood films, her lesbianism is dependent upon visual codes such as stereotypes, visual associations with deviance through camera angle, lighting, dress, etc., or her disruptive, menacing narrative function.

The character of Miss Fellowes (Grayson Hall) in *Night of the Iguana* (John Huston, 1964) offers a good example of how lesbian codes in the cinema operate. First, she perfectly fits the third of the three major lesbian stereotypes that Caroline Sheldon has named, that of the neurotic, closeted lesbian. Her very name not only defines her marital status, her association with masculinity, and the impossibility for intimacy (by the lack of a first name), but also, like Sister George, embodies a gender contradiction, suggesting that she is at odds with herself. She serves both as narrative obstacle to the uneasy heterosexual coupling of the film's main characters (Richard Burton and Ava Gardner) and as counterpoint to underscore Ava Gardner's 'natural', unrepressed expression of (hetero)sexuality.

Most of all, in *Night of the Iguana*, Miss Fellowes's lesbianism is established as deviance through the juxtaposition of her 'artificial' visual image with the film's 'natural' setting. One of its initial scenes shows the film's anti-hero, Shannon (Richard Burton), as a tour guide in Mexico on a bus filled with a women's church group, of which Miss Fellowes is the self-appointed leader. From the bus we are given a view of young Mexican children playing together in a river. Miss Fellowes asks (off-screen, in a voice-over), 'What are we stopping for?' and Shannon answers, 'A moment of beauty, Miss Fellowes. A fleeting glimpse into the lost world of innocence.' Alternately we are shown Shannon looking and the object of his look, establishing a relationship between Shannon and this image of 'nature' (while establishing Miss Fellowes as outside of nature), but also uniting the gaze of the film spectator to the controlling gaze of the only white male character, appreciating the 'exoticism' of racial and sexual otherness from the safety of his tour bus. Miss Fellowes doesn't visually appear on screen until she disrupts the scene by saying, 'Drive on, driver.'

The film simultaneously constructs heterosexuality as 'natural' and homosexuality as 'unnatural'. While the flat tire on the bus is being repaired, Shannon and Charlotte, a young blonde girl on the tour, go swimming. The idyllic image of them holding hands in the water naturalizes the heterosexual bond, and places the image with which it is intercut in sharp relief: Miss Fellowes in a prim skirt and blouse, handbag on her arm, face distorted, screaming on the beach for Charlotte to come back to shore. Her words reveal that she envies this heterosexual bond and is impotent in the face of it: 'You only got to come on this trip because of me! . . . Stay away from that man! . . . ' At the close of the scene, she reaffirms Shannon's 'natural' status, crying, 'you beast, you beast'.

The ideological axis on which the film is built is not the familiar polarization of nature/culture, but rather natural/unnatural, in which nature is elevated to a god, as Shannon articulates in an impromptu sermon later in the film. Language, therefore, as part of culture, is not placed in opposition to nature, but to the unnatural. The connection between language and nature is established through Shannon's sermon which he gives informally in the open air rather than in the artificial, hypocritical church which has de-frocked him. The connection is reinforced by the nature poetry of Nonno, an old man staying at the hacienda, and the simple 'truths' spoken by Miss Jenks, Nonno's granddaughter, all of which function as intermediaries to god/nature. Thus, while lesbianism is established as outside of nature, lesbian desire is positioned outside of language.

One key scene points up the impossibility of articulating lesbian desire within the discourse of the dominant cinema. As Charlotte slips away to seduce Shannon, the film cuts to Miss Fellowes in bed, smiling, talking softly to Charlotte and asking her to forgive her behavior earlier on the beach. Of course, only the film's audience is listening (and therefore this one scene allows for a moment of sympathy, but not identification, with the lesbian character); when Miss Fellowes finally looks over to Charlotte's bed there is no one there to answer her sweet apology or return her gaze. She then sits up rigidly, expressing both anger and betrayal. Her desire, to the extent it has surfaced, is met with absence, and with the omnipotence of heterosexuality which has lured Charlotte away.

But her desire hasn't really surfaced after all. It remains subtextual, barely perceived by either character or audience. To the extent that

Miss Fellowes's desire is articulated through language, its definition is provided solely by others and then only in terms of deviance. When Shannon first arrives at the hacienda of his old friend Maxine Falk (Ava Gardner) and describes to her his situation – that the women's church group in his care is trying to have him fired from the tour company – he mentions that the young girl, Charlotte, is 'traveling under the wing, the military escort, of a butch vocal teacher'. Shannon, perhaps because of his own status as a 'failed man', will go no further, but Maxine Falk later tries to name the source of Miss Fellowes's inhumanity: 'Did you know, if it wasn't for the dykes, the plains of Texas would be engulfed by the gulf!' Shannon tries to stop her, but she continues, 'Let's level for a while, butch ole gal. You know what you're sore about, what you're really sore about, is that little quail of yours has a natural preference for men!'

In the foreground of the shot, Maxine Falk and Miss Fellowes face each other, the former looking unafraid, earthy and sexual, the latter rigid, with her severe features accentuated. In this confrontation between female heterosexuality and lesbianism, heterosexuality gloriously triumphs and the lesbian character retreats. Miss Fellowes averts her eyes in the direction of Shannon, deferring for the first time to his male authority. She asks him innocently, 'What is she talking about?' and he protects her, telling her gently to 'just go, Miss Fellowes, just go', even though her departure from the hotel with the women's church group in tow means his professional ruin. Her departure also means the heterosexual order can be restored; the film's final shot shows Maxine and Shannon together in the foreground, framed by a window with a spectacular view of nature, the ocean and islands, surrounding them. When Maxine confronts Shannon for not letting her 'tell that old dame off', Shannon responds, 'Miss Fellowes is a highly moral person. If she ever recognized the truth about herself, it would destroy her.' Although Shannon saves her from this fate, she is still punished at this moment by being permanently banished from the narrative. And as Vito Russo succinctly put it, 'unconscious lesbianism is its own punishment'.[33]

In most adaptations of Tennessee Williams's plays to the screen, the already obscure homosexual references have been further obscured beyond recognition. Here, however, the representation of Miss Fellowes seems to be surprisingly consistent with Williams's original portrait. As literary scholar John M. Clum points out, Williams's dramas reveal a kind of 'dual vision that shaped his presentation of the homosexuality he was always impelled to write about'.[34] This dual vision, characterized by Williams himself as 'something cloudy, something clear' (the title of one of his plays), 'defines the internal conflict that compelled him to write of . . . homosexuality and, in doing so, to rely on the language of indirection and homophobic discourse'.[35] But while Williams's 'internal conflict' may have resulted in a reliance on homophobic discourse, which is certainly present in *Night of the Iguana*, it can also be argued that this conflict may have worked for as well as against him, by empowering his most interesting and disturbing work, and giving him a greater sensitivity to the complexities of the human heart. Regardless of which interpretation one accepts (and they are not mutually exclusive), Williams prepared the groundwork for the screen character of Miss Fellowes, but she is not merely a product of the script (which Williams did not write) or of the stage play on which it was based. Instead, the film stands as a classic example of how the dominant cinema itself works to construct lesbianism as deviance. Cinematic processes such as the framing and composition of the image, lighting, and the juxtaposition of images and sound through editing, as well as those qualities that the cinema shares with such other forms as drama and fiction, of narrative, character, and dialogue, combine to create 'homophobic discourse' and to naturalize and thereby fortify the heterosexual order.

But it would be wrong to suggest that homophobic discourse is either intrinsic to cinematic processes (see chapters five and six on women's cinema) or must take the form of constructing homosexuality as deviance. Representation changes over time, and there are complex historical reasons why lesbian representation appears as it does in particular historical moments. These reasons become somewhat easier to find when this representation changes drastically, as it did in the 1970s and 1980s, in response to the advent of the gay and women's liberation movements in the late 1960s and early 70s, their radical critiques of the dominant culture and their articulation of alternative visions. In this period, the Hollywood lesbian virtually ceased to be modeled on deviance; she became attractive instead of frightening or ridiculous, and associated with nature instead of with the unnatural.

Of course, frightening, ridiculous and unnatural representations persisted, and even increased – contributing to a backlash against the gay and feminist movements – in the less 'enlightened' films of the 1970s and early 1980s, such as in *Windows* (1980) and in the vampire films discussed in the following chapter. But the prevalent representation of lesbianism which emerged in the 1970s and 80s incorporated ideas and values of the gay and women's movements into a safe, non-threatening framework. This process

73

can best be understood in terms of the workings of cultural hegemony, whereby the dominant culture, rather than relying on direct repression, is able to absorb into its ideological framework the political or cultural definitions of less powerful groups. According to Jackson Lears, through this process, 'Newer values, which sometimes seem potentially subversive at first, are frequently sanitized and incorporated into the mainstream of enlightened opinion.'[36] By assimilating these values, the dominant culture co-opts and disempowers them while it also legitimizes itself as flexible, liberal, and enlightened.

Linda Williams, in her excellent critique of *Personal Best* (Robert Towne, 1982), argues that in the 1970s and 80s the sexual currency of women's bodies changed, and the form of representation constructed within the film corresponds with this change. Male desire now defined a new androgynous feminine ideal, discarding the once fashionable style of passive voluptuousness for sleek active bodies, preferably shown in movement.[37] Elizabeth Ellsworth, writing in *Wide Angle* about feminist responses to *Personal Best*, attempts to provide an explanation for this change. She finds that by 1982, the dominant media had launched a campaign redefining female beauty in a way that seemed to accept but actually thwarted feminist initiatives of the 1970s and early 80s against oppressive media representations which objectified women's bodies.[38] Ellsworth cites as evidence of this co-optation campaign a *Time* magazine August 1982 cover story on the new ideal of feminine beauty, which ' . . . presum[es] to speak to women in an attempt to define women to themselves, from a position that attempts to repulse feminist initiatives in this area by sexualizing women's strength and "physicality" in the service of male pleasure.'[39]

The female imagery offered by *Personal Best* responds to changes in audience expectations. It capitalizes not only on heterosexual men's then-current fascination with the androgynous feminine ideal, but also on women's (and some men's) interest in women and sports, and feminists' interest in the representation of physically active, strong women as well as of a lesbian relationship. But if the sports and lesbian themes have moved to center screen in the attempt to turn these particular audience interests into box office sales, black women athletes remain in the corners of the frame, used as local color to add to the film's 'authenticity'. And, if feminists have been attracted by the film's focus on physically active women, they also have been consistently disappointed, by the voyeuristic cinematography which bombards the viewer with close-up fragmented body parts in 'the current style of fashionably fetishized female bodies

Grayson Hall as the "unnatural woman" in *Night of the Iguana*.

Personal Best: lesbianism is now fashionable.

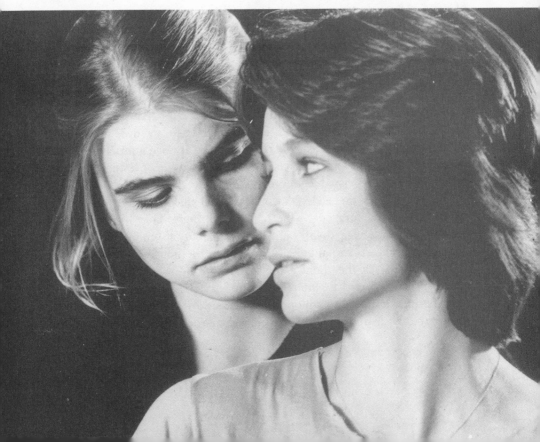

constructed to the measure of male desire'.[40] In an interview in the *Soho News*, director Robert Towne 'justified' the obsessive use of 'crotch shots' by describing his relationship to the image, not as its creator but as its (heterosexual male) consumer: 'I like looking at their thighs. I adore them. I want to fuck the daylights out of them . . . '[41]

The film's fetishization of women's bodies is integrally related to its lesbian plot. It makes safe the threat of lesbianism and of physically strong, active women, and puts them both in the service of male sexual fantasy. In the 1960s, the representation of lesbianism, particularly the visual image of a Miss Fellowes or Sister George, with her asexual, deviant and grotesque associations, would clearly resist such a sexual function. However, even these earlier films exploited the voyeuristic potential that lesbianism holds for heterosexual men; film critic Andrew Sarris thoroughly enjoyed the lesbian sex scene in *The Killing of Sister George* because through watching it 'we participate in the seduction of an attractive woman [Childie, played by Susannah York].'[42] By the 1980s, the 'deviant' butch was gone and her passive femme no longer held the same erotic appeal for men. Styles of female desirability had changed.

But so had the long-standing tension between theories of lesbianism as gender inversion and as object choice (described in chapter one). Although Krafft-Ebing's original preoccupation with lesbianism as a form of gender inversion persisted throughout the twentieth century in the popular imagination and re-surfaced in the post-war cinema as the 'butch' or 'mannish woman' stereotype, Havelock Ellis's no less sinister theories about lesbianism as an insidious, acquired condition, involving a female object choice rather than a rejection of femaleness, also persisted and in the 1970s and 80s gained dominance.

In 1982 both lesbian characters of *Personal Best*, Tory (Patrice Donnelly) and Chris (Mariel Hemingway), are represented as attractive, sexual and active women, with strong, sleek bodies that are at once androgynous (as are their names) and feminine. Unlike a representation of lesbianism that depends upon the visual codes of gender inversion, these 'feminine' images easily lend themselves to heterosexual male fantasy. Such fantasy is further encouraged by the narrative through Tory's reference to her former relationships with (and thus availability to) men, and Chris's conversion to heterosexuality halfway through the film.

If the film uses the themes of lesbianism and women in sports to appeal to male voyeuristic interests, many lesbian spectators are still able to find it pleasurable through oppositional viewing strategies. This comes through clearly in a sociological study of lesbian spectators' responses to the film as well as an analysis of film reviews in the lesbian press.[43] Comparing liberal-, socialist-, and lesbian-feminist reviews, Elizabeth Ellsworth has found that non-lesbian reviews admired such qualities as the absence of stereotypes and the achievement of women in a predominantly male field, but these reviews did not alter and rearrange stylistic and formal elements of the film to generate alternative meanings. On the other hand, 'lesbian feminist reviewers launched the most radical rewriting of the film ... ' in order 'to find pleasure and objects for illicit desire in that which is most threatening to dominant sexual politics'.[44] Specifically, her study of lesbian film reviews of *Personal Best* reveals that many reviewers imagined or fantasized an ending other than appears on screen; they ignored long sequences which focused on heterosexual romance; they altered narrative events to make it possible to read the film as a validation of lesbianism; and they redefined the 'main character' and 'supporting character' so that rather than focus on Mariel Hemingway, who is given much more screen time, they focus on Patrice Donnelly as the more 'convincing' lesbian and therefore the more appropriate 'object of desire'.

Through an informal survey of forty-four women who saw *Personal Best* in theaters in Chicago, Chris Straayer confirmed Ellsworth's findings that lesbian audiences reversed the star hierarchy, so that Tory (Patrice Donnelly) was the 'real star' of the movie.[45] Straayer reports that self-defined 'lesbian-feminists' had a bittersweet enjoyment of the film because of their discomfort with its sexism and heterosexism, and because the relationship between Chris and Tory did not ring true to their own experience. One woman wrote,

> I saw no evidence of love between the two women. I was especially shocked during the car fight when Tory said they fucked each other. I've never heard a lesbian use that word to describe her love-making.

According to Straayer, 'By far, the most frequent and emphatic comment was a dissatisfaction with the portrayal of Chris and Tory's relationship', specifically because the two characters never discussed the relationship and no lesbian context was created for it. And, indeed, the film, per- haps under the guise of 'tolerance', does create a certain unexamined, taken-for-granted attitude about the relationship which to many lesbians would seem implausible. This attitude is key to the ideological processes at work in the film.

Most striking about *Personal Best*, coming as it does after a series of Hollywood films of the 1970s and 80s that focus on heterosexual female friendship (*Julia, Girlfriends, The Turning Point*) and that often

77

use lesbianism as a boundary of deviance over which this friendship will not cross, is the way in which lesbianism is constructed as a 'natural' phenomenon, and the sexual relationship is a 'natural' outgrowth of, rather than a threat to, women's friendship.[46] It's so natural as never to warrant explanation or even direct mention by the lovers, except in one scene which points up clearly how sexuality is positioned in male terms: when Tory defines their three-year relationship as 'friends who fuck once in a while'. Sexual desire is not accentuated but rather minimized and naturalized by the film's processes, and lesbianism is thus represented as a non-threatening alternative to heterosexuality (only for the alternative to be rejected in the course of the narrative). The liberal ideology of the film can therefore appeal to some feminist and progressive audiences, by offering lesbianism as an attractive alternative, but one that can never succeed. Liberal heterosexuals can rest assured that their identification with heterosexuality is not compulsory but, as Chris's is, freely chosen and hence the superior choice.

As in *Silkwood*, the relationship of Tory to Chris is that of mother to daughter. Tory is older and more experienced; she initiates the relationship and provides maternal care and support. As Linda Williams sees it,

> This mothering is the real impediment to the growth and endurance of their relationship. Yet this mothering also renders the relationship safe in the eyes of the film's ultimately patriarchal system of values. The film can afford to celebrate nostalgically the sensual lost Eden of a female-to-female bond precisely because it chooses to depict this bond as the non-viable pre-Oedipal dependence and narcissistic identification of mother and daughter.[47]

Such a mother/daughter relationship is of course 'natural', and within this framework so is Chris's eventual transference to the 'father', the man with whom she becomes romantically involved. The representation of lesbianism as a pre-Oedipal regression to be overcome marks a considerable change: from associations with deviance and the unnatural in the 1960s, to more acceptable sensual and romantic associations in Hollywood films of the past decade. Lesbianism has come to represent a natural, innocent, but in the end impossible world.

This move from deviant to natural continues with *The Color Purple* (Steven Spielberg, 1985) which, like *Personal Best*, appealed to changes in certain audience expectations in the 1970s and 80s. But while *Personal Best* moved lesbianism to center screen, leaving black women in the margins, *The Color Purple* moved black women to center screen and relegated lesbianism to the margins.[48] The joke in lesbian circles while the film was in production was that Steven Spielberg wasn't intimidated by creatures from outer space but a lesbian relationship was more than he could handle. Unfortunately, the film does 'handle' lesbianism all too carefully, so that rather than erase the lesbianism in the novel, which is what it seems to do at first glance, the film provides a subtle, ingenious transformation of its meaning.

In the course of Alice Walker's novel, its narrator, Celie, a poor black woman, finds her own voice and in so doing rejects patriarchal ideology. This movement from voicelessness within patriarchy to female transgression and empowerment is the drive of the narrative, and yet it is missing altogether from the film which instead upholds hegemonic values. Molly Hite draws attention to how Steven Spielberg

> ... felt it necessary to reinscribe the law of the father, dismantled entirely in the book, by providing Shug with a wholly gratuitous 'daddy', both a biological father and a Christian minister (and thus emissary of the great white father whom Walker's Shug dismissed during the course of the speech that provides the book with its title) ... Spielberg unerringly provides climax and denouement by restoring the patriarchal status quo.[49]

The color purple in the novel refers, on one level, to a field of flowers, symbolizing a rejection of God as a white male authority, and transforming 'him' into 'flowers, wind, water, a big rock', a non-patriarchal spiritual force. Drawing on a long association between lesbianism and the colors violet and lavender, the color purple also refers to lesbianism, specifically sex between Celie and Shug, which in the context of this discussion about religion is listed as one of the blessings which God loves. Michele Wallace, in her essay 'Blues for Mr. Spielberg' sees the book's metaphor (but not the film's) as bringing together these religious and sexual meanings:

> The traditional image of God as a stern, elderly white patriarch is reconceived as the cushy inside of a clitoral orgasm, the appreciation of the color purple . . .[50]

The film, however, not only rejects this reconceptualizing of God in non-patriarchal terms, but also rejects the novel's use of lesbianism and female orgasm as important steps to Celie's self-esteem as an adult woman. Instead, purple is the field in which Celie and Nettie play as children, and the adult lesbian relationship in the novel, between Shug and Celie, is reformulated in the film as a childhood experience: the sensual, 'innocent' sisterly love between Celie and Nettie.

Early in the film we are introduced to Celie and Nettie as children, and in their clothing and movements they are visually paired. They sing a song about how as sisters 'me and you must never part'; their love is 'naturalized' by its familial and childhood context. The 'man', their father, disrupts their sororal bliss by literally coming between them and prying them apart. The excessive emotion with which this separation occurs pushes the film into full-fledged melodrama, so that we can mourn this action while at the same time accepting it as also 'natural', a harsh but necessary step in their development into adult women who must take their proper places in the patriarchy.

Celie's lesbian relationship with the sexual Shug is minimized in favor of Celie's sororal longing for Nettie, and in fact the former can best be characterized as an inadequate substitute for the latter. Whereas Celie and Nettie are narcissistically paired, Celie and Shug are positioned as polar opposites. In the juke joint Shug sings a song written for Celie which mostly features the words, 'sister, we're two of a kind', words that define Celie's relationship with Nettie but hardly with Shug. In the next scene Celie wears Shug's clothes, which mitigates their huge visual difference, but still the two are contrasted by Shug's confidence and Celie's shyness, and by Celie's simple comment that 'He beat me for not being you'. The visual and narrative contrasting of Shug and Celie doesn't necessarily preclude the possibility of lesbian desire (in fact, in most lesbian narratives of the 1980s, visual contrasts between women are erotically charged), but it does preclude it in a film which reduces lesbian desire to the narcissistic sororal longing of children. This one scene in which Celie puts on Shug's clothes in an attempt to be more like her alludes vaguely to their sexual relationship. Shug starts to kiss Celie, at first in a maternal sort of way, and Celie responds like an embarrassed child. They start to embrace, the camera moves in for a close-up of Celie's hand on Shug's shoulder and, so much for revealing the cushy insides of orgasms, the camera retreats to some windchimes and the scene ends.

But it is not only the avoidance of the sexual scene that undermines the spectator's ability to view Shug and Celie's relationship in terms of lesbianism. In the departure scene that follows shortly after this allusion to a sexual relationship, Shug leaves without even looking back at Celie. When she returns to the screen a few scenes later, she defines their relationship in terms of men: 'We're married, two married ladies now.' The one time that the differences between them disappear is when Shug stops Celie from killing Mister with his razor. Shug grabs Celie from behind and holds her

Robert Towne, director of *Personal Best*: "I like looking at their thighs. I adore them. I want to fuck the daylights out of them."

The Color Purple: Shug begins to seduce a frightened Celie, before the film replaces lesbian passion with windchimes.

close, and the figures of the two women are romantically matched. This image could be seen as sexual, but ironically, Shug's physical closeness with Celie is in the service of continuing Celie's enslavement to Mister.

Toward the end of the film, Celie's voice-over tells us that rather than a radical transformation, such as Alice Walker's Celie undergoes, 'the more things change, the more they stay the same. Me and Shug, her smile, but us still longing'. Shug is longing for a reconciliation with her father and, in the broader sense, with the patriarchy. Celie is longing for Nettie and, as Linda Williams noted of *Personal Best,* for 'the lost Eden of the female-to-female bond' of childhood, which becomes both non-viable and mythic in adulthood. If *Personal Best* frames lesbian desire in the context of female adolescence, as a temporary stage in coming to sexual awareness, *The Color Purple* transforms this desire into nostalgia for an earlier stage of sexual development. In intercut scenes of Nettie's life in Africa, we see two girls repeating Nettie and Celie's childhood patterns, rendering this relationship universal, ahistorical, and most of all 'natural'. The racist association of blacks with nature, as being 'inferior' humans and therefore closer to animals, operates in both the American and African settings, further emphasizing this association of 'lesbian' desire with a natural, idyllic state of being.

Using the codes of Hollywood melodrama, Nettie and Celie are reunited in the film's end, running as if in a Clairol commercial into each other's arms. But they are adults now, and their narcissistic longing for each other must be replaced with a more 'appropriate' relationship, in which their complex ties to each other have a collaborative rather than subversive function within the larger patriarchal family. No longer visually paired, the sisters are now visually contrasted, with Celie's American identity serving as counterpoint for Nettie's exoticism as an African woman. Despite the emotional strings the ending pulls through their reunion, Nettie and Celie cannot enact their dream of childhood paradise. As old women they replay their girlhood game that opened the film. And yet as they are beautifully silhouetted against the big yellow sun, the shadow of Mister walks across the screen behind them, and the sororal bond is once again (this time visually rather than narratively) overshadowed and disrupted by the figure of the patriarchy.

Deviant and 'unnatural' lesbian characters of the 1950s and 60s have given way, temporarily at least, to those who pine after utopian sisterly love, although neither is ever allowed a happy ending. The exception, of course, is *Desert Hearts* (Donna Deitch, US, 1985), which rejects both of these models and permits the relationship to be both sexual and open-ended. Directed by a woman and based on the lesbian novel by Jane Rule, *Desert Hearts* is a lesbian Western with all the visual trappings of Hollywood. However, Deitch raised the financing and produced the film herself – a ten-year saga – and it is this independent financial status which has allowed the film a way out from the Hollywood unnatural/natural dilemma.

But even given Hollywood's limited alternatives (and also given the steady decline in the quality of the movies since the advent of television), lesbians can and do find pleasure in the mainstream cinema. Lesbian images are still rare enough to be poignant whenever and however they do occur. Today, looking back to the films that represent lesbianism as deviance, it is possible to utilize these images in the service of camp. In the more recent films that naturalize lesbian desire, but offer it as an alternative that is not viable within the 'real' world of the film's fiction, lesbians can either invent their own narratives that allow the lesbianism to be enacted or can become engaged with the film through an attraction to one of the characters. (If all else fails, there is always the girl sitting next to you in the theater.) For all its disappointments – and for lesbians there are many – the magic of the cinema keeps us coming back.

4

The Vampire Lovers

Lesbians are sharks, vampires, creatures from the deep lagoon, godzillas, hydrogen bombs, inventions of the laboratory, werewolves – all of whom stalk Beverly Hills by night. Christopher Lee, in drag, in the Hammer Films, middle period, is my ideal lesbian.

Bertha Harris, 'What is a Lesbian?'[1]

D racula, that tall, dark, handsome menace, has been given some stiff competition over the years by an even more attractive female counterpart – the lesbian vampire. She has found an enthusiastic medium for visual expression in the cinema, which has resurrected lesbian vampire tales dating far back in literature and legend.

Merging two kinds of sexual outlaws, the lesbian vampire is more than simply a negative stereotype. She is a complex and ambiguous figure, at once an image of death and an object of desire, drawing on profound subconscious fears that the living have toward the dead and that men have toward women, while serving as a focus for repressed fantasies. The generic vampire image both expresses and represses sexuality, but the lesbian vampire especially operates in the sexual rather than the supernatural realm.

The English-language films considered here are but a small sampling of the many horror films that feature female vampires with lesbian tendencies. The scope and persistence of this phenomenon should not be underestimated; outside of male pornography, the lesbian vampire is the most persistent lesbian image in the history of the cinema. The lesbian vampire films cover six decades of film history, from the 1930s to the 1980s; their countries of origin include the United States, Great Britain, France, West Germany, Belgium, Spain, and Italy. The European films, with such titles as *Vampyros Lesbos – Die Erbin des Dracula* (Jess Franco, Germany/Spain, 1971) and *La Novia Ensangrentada* or *The Blood-Spattered Bride* (Aranda, Spain, 1972), sound enticing, yet must await further study.

In the early 1960s Barbara Steele played a vampire in a number of Italian films with lesbian overtones including *Black Sunday* (Mario Bava, 1960), a film which influenced the screenwriter of the English lesbian vampire films produced a decade later, and *Castle of Blood* or *La Danza Macabra* (Anthonio Margheriti, 1963), in which Steele's character kills her lesbian cousin and lover (Margaret Robsham). Jean Rollin directed a series of surrealist French horror films, including *Le Viol du Vampire* (1967), *La Vampire Nue* (1969), *Le Frisson des Vampires* (1970), and *Vierges et Vampires* (1971), all of which sacrificed narrative coherence for shocking sado-masochistic lesbian images. Rollin's iconography features leather and metal chains, spikes protruding from women's breasts, scenes of gang rape, and vampires reduced to drinking from their own veins.

Such jarring imagery departs significantly from that of the typical, more romantic lesbian vampire film, which has certain fairly consistent characteristics: Gothic themes and imagery, large empty castles and dark, romantic landscapes, and the arrival, early in the film, of a mysterious, aristocratic figure. With a few exceptions, these horror films were made on very small budgets, with extremely low production values. Their low budget look gives them an exaggerated, camp quality, which for viewers today is often their redeeming feature. They were originally shown in second-rate commercial movie houses or in drive-in theaters, and now a number of them have been resurrected on the home video market.

The association of vampirism with lesbianism is far-reaching and long-lived. As Richard Dyer has pointed out, the literary images of each are closely related and often described in the same morbid language.[2] For example, in the 1915 novel, *Regiment of Women* by Winifred Ashton (pseud. Clemence Dane), the following description is not of a vampire's victim but of one woman who has fallen in love with another: 'So thin – she's growing so dreadfully thin. Her neck! You should see her neck – salt-cellars, literally! And she had such a beautiful neck! . . . And so white and listless.'

The connection between lesbians and vampires has not been restricted to the horror genre, but resonates throughout much of the existing cultural representations of lesbianism. In a number of European art films of the 1960s and 70s, such as Ingmar Bergman's *Persona* (Sweden, 1965) and Rainer Werner Fassbinder's *The Bitter Tears of Petra von Kant* (West Germany, 1972), vampirism is suggested through the erotic relationship between two women, in which one woman takes over the personality or soul of the other. Susan Sontag has described the elusive plot of *Persona* as 'two women bound together in a passionate agonized relation-

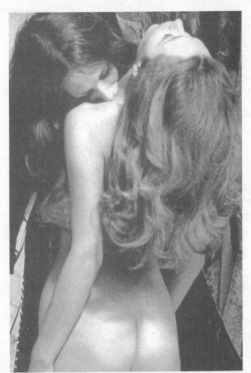

Sado-masochistic lesbian vampires from Jean Rollin's surrealist horror films.
Below right: Stephanie Rothman creates a "feminist" vampire in her B-movie,
The Velvet Vampire (1971).

ship' which 'is rendered mythically as vampirism: at one point, Alma sucks Elizabeth's blood'.[3]

Lillian Faderman in *Surpassing the Love of Men* finds that a spate of lesbian vampire novels appeared in the first half of the twentieth century. Vampire imagery serves as a metaphor for lesbianism in such books as Francis Brett Young's *White Ladies* (1935) and Dorothy Baker's *Trio* (1943), and *Vampir* (1932), which was published in Germany under the author's anagram Ano Nymous. Faderman connects the emergence of lesbianism as vampirism to the pathologizing of women's relationships by medical and cultural authorities. The vampire metaphor, Faderman asserts, served to enforce the transition from nineteenth-century socially accepted close female relationships to the redefinition of such relationships as deviant in the first half of the twentieth century.[4]

Although the lesbian vampire image resurfaced in this period, its origins can be traced back to several earlier sources of vampire lore. The most significant of these is the Victorian novel *Carmilla* (1871) by J. Sheridan Le Fanu, which predates Bram Stoker's *Dracula* by twenty-five years. The fictional Carmilla is an aristocratic noblewoman, the Countess Millarca Karnstein, who reappears as a vampire a hundred and fifty years after her physical death. It is a typical Victorian novel: genteel on the surface, but beneath is the darker side of the spirit. Laura, Carmilla's 'victim', describes her vampire lover in romantic terms:

> [Carmilla] used to place her pretty arms around my neck, draw me to her, and laying her cheek next to mine, murmur with her lips near my ear, 'Dearest, your little heart is wounded; think me not cruel because I obey the irresistible law of my strength and weakness; if your dear heart is wounded, my wild heart bleeds with yours.

Carmilla falls in love with her so-called victims; she is characterized sympathetically in that she acts out of compulsion rather than malice. Gene Damon, writing in the early American lesbian publication *The Ladder*, claimed that the novel *Carmilla* has 'long been a sub-basement Lesbian classic' but the film based on it, *The Vampire Lovers*, is 'a male movie, for a male audience'.[5] What has survived of *Carmilla* from Victorian literature and worked its way into twentieth-century cinema is its muted expression of lesbianism, no longer sympathetically portrayed but now reworked into a male pornographic fantasy.

Although in the earliest lesbian vampire film, *Dracula's Daughter* (Lambert Hillyer, 1936), the sexuality of the vampire (Gloria Holden) is discreetly implied, by the late 1960s and early 70s, lesbian sexual behavior had become graphically depicted, another titillating, exaggerated characteristic of the excessive B-movie genre. One obvious explanation for this change in representation is the gradual relaxation of the strict censorship laws in the United States and Great Britain in the mid-1960s, which these films further encouraged. No longer hunted by censors, some twenty or more lesbian vampires could be found stalking the silver screen between the years of 1970 and 1974 alone. In the early 1970s, Hammer Studio in Great Britain released its trilogy of X-rated 'sexploitation flicks': *The Vampire Lovers* (Roy Baker, 1970), *Twins of Evil* (John Hough, 1971) and *Lust for a Vampire* (Jimmy Sangster, 1971). *The Vampire Lovers* establishes the narrative formula that subsequent films, with slight deviations, take up, and helps define the genre by fully exploiting the pornographic value of the relationship between the vampire and her victim.

This pornographic appeal was a strong motivation for producing most of these films in the first place. Tudor Gates, the screenwriter of the Hammer trilogy, claims that with these films Hammer Studio was deliberately challenging the British Board of Film Censors on the question of where to draw the line on allowable representation.[6] By the early 1970s, graphic sexual imagery that elsewhere would be excised by censors was considered more acceptable within the realm of the supernatural. As the 1970s wore on, this imagery became increasingly possible in other forms of cinema, and the lesbian vampire was no longer necessary to circumvent censorship regulations. Still, the figure didn't completely disappear; she continued to hold an erotic power and fascination beyond her purely pornographic value. Although on the decline since the mid-1970s, it is in her nature to return again.

The Hammer Studio films are invariably set in an ambiguous, mythologized past, when strict gender roles demanded that men be brave and women helpless. Yet the films' production unmistakably belongs to the late 1960s and early 70s, a period in which such clear cut definitions of masculinity and femininity were increasingly coming under fire. Bonnie Zimmerman, writing in *Jump Cut* in 1981, speculates on the relationship between the sudden appeal of the lesbian vampire in 1970 and the initial gains of the feminist movement. She writes,

Although direct parallels between social forces and popular culture are risky at best, the popularity of the lesbian vampire film in the early 1970s may be related to the beginnings of an international feminist movement ... Since feminism between 1970 and 1973 was not

Hammer Film Studio's *Lust for a Vampire:* Before and After photos.

yet perceived as a fundamental threat, men could enjoy the sexual thrill provided by images of lesbian vampires stealing women and sometimes destroying men in the process. The creators of those images – like the pornographic filmmakers who appeal to male fantasies with scenes of lesbianism – must have felt secure enough in their power and that of their primarily male audience to flirt with lesbianism and female violence against men.[7]

But a reconsideration of this lesbian vampire popularity more strongly suggests that what the creators of these images must have felt secure about was not so much their male power as the potential box office returns on a low budget exploitation product. It was, in fact, the huge financial success of *The Vampire Lovers* that motivated Hammer Studios to continue with their lesbian theme. The relationship which Zimmerman seeks to establish between the early 1970s feminist movement and the appearance of so many lesbian vampire films rests not on the security but on the insecurity that the feminist movement generated in male spectators at that time. Feminists were angrily demanding sexual autonomy from men and control over their own bodies. Strengthened by participation in consciousness-raising groups, many women across the United States and in Europe demanded sexual pleasure and sexual equality with their husbands and boyfriends, and many more left these men and proclaimed their lesbianism. Under such circumstances, men understandably felt their dominant social position to be dangerously threatened.

Although psychic fears and historical circumstances rarely coincide so directly or neatly, and it would be reductive to explain the former as solely the product of the latter, the emergence of the lesbian vampire in this period does, in some measure, symbolize this threat. The lesbian vampire provokes and articulates anxieties in the heterosexual male spectator, only for the film to quell these anxieties and reaffirm his maleness through the vampire's ultimate destruction. The lesbian vampire is at once attractive and threatening to men, in part because she expresses an active sexual desire, something which men may fantasize about safely in the cinema even while threatened by its prospect at home.

While sexually active, the lesbian vampire is still visually coded as feminine: she has long hair, large breasts, pale white skin, and wears floor-length, translucent dresses. Unlike the 'masculine' images of lesbians in more mainstream films of the late Sixties and early Seventies – *The Fox* (Mark Rydell, 1966), *The Killing of Sister George* (Robert Aldrich, 1968), for example – the lesbian vampire fits the stereotype, not of the mannish lesbian, but of the white, feminine heterosexual woman. Her vampirism, therefore, is doubly disturbing, as she appears 'normal' by society's standards for women and yet is not. James Donald has noted that 'works of the fantastic insist upon the delusory nature of perception' and 'play . . . upon the insecurity of the boundaries between the "I" and the "not-I" . . .'[8] The vampire's femininity contributes to this insecurity by her ability to 'pass' as heterosexual; she is not visually identifiable as either lesbian or vampire.

The lesbian vampire not only crosses boundaries (through passing), but breaks down boundaries between the male 'I' and the female 'not-I' as well. While appearing to be excessively 'feminine', she also contradicts and confounds this femininity through the anxious attention focused on her mouth. Christopher Craft, in his illuminating study of Bram Stoker's *Dracula*, describes the vampire's mouth as follows:

As the primary site of erotic experience . . . this mouth equivocates, giving the lie to the easy separation of the masculine and the feminine. Luring at first with an inviting orifice, a promise of red softness, but delivering instead a piercing bone, the vampire mouth fuses and confuses . . . the gender-based categories of the penetrating and the receptive. With its soft flesh barred by hard bone, its red crossed by white, this mouth compels opposites and contrasts into a frightening unity.[9]

Medical case histories in the early twentieth century reveal deep anxieties about the possibility of female penetration. Ridiculously imposing a heterosexual model of sexual behavior onto lesbian desire, medical 'experts' actually attempted to measure imagined 'deformity' of lesbians' genitalia and their possibilities for sexual penetration.[10] In the lesbian vampire story, this anxiety has been displaced and refocused on the mouth, another 'feminine' sexual orifice which combines the 'masculine' ability to penetrate, via the teeth. Thus the vampire embodies age-old popular fears of women which have been expressed through the image of the 'vagina dentata', the vagina with teeth, the penetrating woman. Jean Rollin's lesbian vampire with spikes protruding from her breasts expresses a similar anxiety.

The fluctuations between desire and fear generated by the vampire seem to require a 'strict, indeed almost schematic formal management of narrative material', as Christopher Craft has demonstrated.[11] This management of narrative material is formulaic: the vampire is first introduced in order to disrupt and invert the 'natural order' and to provoke anxieties in the characters and spectator alike; the vampire then engages in vampirism as entertainment and sexual titillation for the prolonged middle section of the narrative; and finally the vampire is destroyed and the 'natural order' reaffirmed. In the case of the lesbian vampire, a more specific narrative formula is often further imposed upon the generic vampire plot: a lesbian vampire and a mortal man compete for the possession of a woman. In this bisexual triangle, the man is aligned with the forces of good, the vampire with the forces of evil, and the woman whose fate hangs in the balance is usually a 'nice, sweet girl' with no intrinsic moral value attached to her but who is merely a receptacle to assume the values of either one.

This alignment of moral values with specific characters is established at the start. In the Hammer Studio production, *The Vampire Lovers*, the man is shown in relation to church, family and community; Carmilla (Ingrid Pitt) is a stranger with a 'foreign' accent, a newcomer with no community ties. While the man is a moral, proper gentleman and rides a white horse, the vampire is clearly a 'bad girl'. It is this 'bad girl', however, who holds the stronger appeal; Linda Williams has pointed out that 'it is a truism of the horror genre that sexual interest resides most often in the monster [or vampire] and not in the bland ostensible heroes . . . who often prove powerless at the crucial moment.'[12] Carmilla's 'badness' is conveyed through sexual signs: her dress is low-cut, her smile mischievous and seductive, and her body too well developed to confirm the youthful, girlish pose she assumes. The victim, Emma (Madeleine Smith), over whom they compete, is younger, starry-eyed and innocent, and, at least initially, subservient to her father.

While it may be possible for lesbian viewers to derive some pleasure from the vampire's sexual escapades, these scenes invariably cater to male heterosexual fantasy. One particularly explicit scene from *The Vampire Lovers* is a perfect example of male voyeurism and, ultimately, male sadistic impulses. Emma comes into Carmilla's bedroom while Carmilla is taking a bath. First we see Carmilla in a medium shot, eyes averted off screen and naked from the waist up in the bathtub. Her large breasts are center screen and dominate the shot. Then she turns as she rises, and we have a view of her entire torso from the back just as she drapes a towel around her. These two shots underscore the spectator's position as voyeur, able to see her body but fleetingly, before she covers herself, and without meeting her gaze. Carmilla walks to the mirror and sits so that her back is to the camera; we simultaneously see her naked back and, in the mirror reflection, her face, neck, shoulders and breasts (the standard myth that vampires lack a reflection is dispensed with here in the service of prurient interests). Thus, at the moment when the lesbian vampire is about to seduce her victim for the first time, her image is rendered less threatening: it is visually fragmented onto different spatial planes through the framing of the foreground and mirror images. This symbolic dismemberment of her body foreshadows her eventual destruction by the film's end.

In this bedroom scene, Carmilla is telling Emma to borrow one of her dresses, but first to take everything off underneath. Emma's hesitancy, 'What will my father say?' and Carmilla's reassurance, 'He will enjoy it, as all men do', further speaks to the pleasures of the male spectator and establishes the context in which to view what follows. A half-naked Carmilla chases a half-naked Emma around the room, and they land conveniently on the bed. We see them embrace, and then for a moment a lamp in the foreground obstructs our view. This obstruction postpones voyeurism, which is a way of heightening and intensifying voyeuristic pleasure. The bulbous, symmetrical shape of the lamp at once shields our view of the women and symbolically recreates the fetishized breast imagery in the foreground of the shot. Thus voyeurism and fetishism work together in this scene to contain and assuage the threat the vampire poses to the male spectator.

Within the narrative, the vampire represents the threat of violence as well as of sexuality. Usually the vampire seduces rather than attacks her victims; this can be seen as a relatively positive attribute in that the lesbian vampire doesn't seek to destroy her victims, but rather to make them into accomplices. Furthermore, seduction suggests a complicity on the part of the victim, indicating the relationship is mutually desirable to a certain extent. But lest we develop too much admiration for this charming seductress, random and gruesome violence is occasionally added to heighten the sense of perversion and destruction that she embodies. That this violence is often directed at women, for whom the vampire has a distinct sexual preference, serves further to link images of lesbian sexuality to depravity.

It is clear that while the vampires, who are always aristocratic ladies with long family bloodlines, seduce and initiate relationships with other aristocratic ladies, they demonstrate a clear class bias in their seemingly random attacks on and murders of peasants, servant girls, and other lower class women. These mere peasant girls are dispensable in the film's development but the violent attacks on them are not: they serve to unite the titillation and the threat of gratuitous violence.

In a scene from another Hammer Studio film, *Twins of Evil*, one of the two female twins has just become a vampire. As she begins to attack a local peasant girl (chained to the wall), there is a brief, unspoken erotic exchange between the two women: the victim momentarily responds to the vampire's advances and they seem about to kiss, when the vampire attacks. We hear a scream and the shot dissolves into a close-up on the face of a male vampire, previously in the corner of the frame voyeuristically watching the encounter, now laughing wickedly. The lesbian sexual overtones of the violence are pronounced, monitored by the male gaze from the edge of the frame, and confirmed by the laughter that expresses his pleasure in looking. Lesbian scenes from the third film in the Hammer trilogy, *Lust for a Vampire*, are also consistently framed in relation to an on-screen male voyeur: one man watches as two naked women swim and kiss in the moonlight; another listens; calls out and pounds on the door behind which two women make vampiric love.

Blood and Roses, directed by Roger Vadim in 1960, is a film which, unlike the later Hammer Studio productions, avoids the excessive blood and graphic sexual images associated with the genre. Instead it is more closely related to the European art cinema tradition with its emphasis on lush, provocative visual imagery over a straightforward, coherent narrative. In one beautiful scene, the vampire Carmilla (Annette Vadim), attacks Liza, a servant girl. Here it is ambiguous whether the vampire is pursuing sex or violence; the film's visual style barely distinguishes between them. The music, cinemascope pastoral imagery, and moving camera (a slow tracking shot of the two women running through the landscape) contribute to what seems to be, at first, a romantic seduction scene that eventually turns on itself and becomes violent. We don't see the violence, but we see Liza's expression of fear, hear her scream at the end of the scene, and subsequently learn that she is dead. Even in *Blood and Roses*, which avoids the typical exploitation approach, sexuality and violence are visually coupled, as complementary qualities intrinsic to a lesbian relationship.

Another cultural myth to which the lesbian vampire film subscribes, maintains that lesbians are narcissistic. This is most blatant in the use of twins in *Twins of Evil* and in the scene from *The Vampire Lovers* that immediately follows the bedroom scene described earlier. After Carmilla and Emma emerge from the bedroom, they walk down the stairs together with their hair, dress and expressions identical. Whereas previously the difference between them was emphasized (Carmilla older, stronger, aggressive, more sophisticated; Emma younger, weaker, passive, more naive), following the seduction scene they have become narcissistically matched.

Another, related cultural myth asserts that lesbian sexuality is infantile: in the *Twins of Evil* scene described above, the vampire goes not for

Carmilla (Ingrid Pitt) makes her moves on the innocent Emma in *The Vampire Lovers*.

A pastoral scene between vampire and victim in Roger Vadim's "art film" *Blood and Roses*.

the throat, but in a gesture that makes reference to infantile obsession, the victim's breast. There are similar scenes in all of the Hammer Studio productions, in which breast imagery dominates the screen and is given anxious attention through accentuating clothes and symbolic displacement. Both solid and fluid, and representing mother and lover, breasts – like the vampire's mouth – symbolically embrace contradictions. In *Twins of Evil* the breast imagery creates a kind of visual spectacle, to deflect the spectator's attention away from the contradictions generated by the film – the contradictions of constructing an image of active and dangerous female desire which is circumscribed and defined by male spectatorial pleasure. At the same time, the breast fetishism helps reduce lesbian desire to an infantile, pre-Oedipal phase of development.

One way the narrative structure enforces these cultural myths is by closing down the range of possible, alternative interpretations that spectators can read from the film. In *The Vampire Lovers* this is done in part by framing the entire plot of the film with the perspective of a male narrator, a famous vampire hunter, who appears on screen only in the opening and closing sequences and who gives a voice-over narration leading the audience into the film's events. It is interesting that, with this one exception of the male narrator, the entire plot of *The Vampire Lovers* otherwise follows very closely the plot of the Victorian novel *Carmilla*. Screenwriter Tudor Gates recalls that Hammer Studios was able to sell the idea of *The Vampire Lovers* on the basis of a lurid poster and a three page outline, and the outline described this opening scene of the vampire hunter.[13] The male narrator is therefore the screenwriter's pure fabrication, created for the purpose of raising finance but having the additional benefit of enabling male viewers to be sexually aroused by the film with the assurance that the controlling voice of the narrative is male. After his introduction, the film retreats immediately to a detached, impersonal form of address that masks this male subjectivity behind a seemingly objective 'narrative truth'.

An important characteristic of the lesbian vampire is that she relies far more on her sexual powers than on her supernatural powers – in fact her sexual powers are usually equated with supernatural powers. In the early days of the cinema, the word 'vampire' had a meaning similar to 'vamp': a beautiful woman whose sexual desire, if fulfilled, would drain the life blood of man. This mortal vampire was an extremely popular character in early films. The earliest such film was made in 1910 and called *The Vampire*; it was reviewed that year in the *New York Dramatic Mirror* as being about 'a beautiful woman who delighted in ruining men'. Between

The Vampire Lovers: After the sex scene, the vampire (right) and her victim become narcissistically matched.

Twins of Evil: More breast fetishism from Hammer Film Studios.

1914 and 1916, the classic 'vampire' was played by Theda Bara in such films as *A Fool There Was* (1914) and *Sin* (1915). Theda Bara's real name was Theodosia Goodman and she was the daughter of a Jewish garment worker; voluptuous and dark, her image was linked to evil sexuality, helping to define and keep 'pure' the more common blonde virgin image. But if men projected dangerous sexuality on Theda Bara, female spectators could find in her role the pleasure of revenge. Bara herself once said, 'Women are my greatest fans because they see in my [role as] vampire the impersonal vengeance of all their unavenged wrongs ... I have the face of a vampire, perhaps, but the heart of a feministe.'[14] In the first decade of the cinema there were at least forty films about this mortal female vampire, whom men could find sexually enticing while women could fantasize female empowerment.

In the most recent lesbian vampire film, *The Hunger* (1980), the vampire's power is still purely sexual, even though now she is also endowed with supernatural qualities. In a scene famous to lesbian audiences, the sophisticated, aristocratic Catherine Deneuve seduces the more butch Susan Sarandon, and Susan Sarandon is so enticed by the sexual rather than the supernatural that they are already undressed and well under way before we are reminded, through images of a blood exchange, that one of the women is a vampire.

As a measure of this scene's importance to lesbian spectators, a debate has been generated within lesbian circles as to the 'authenticity' of the sex between Deneuve and Sarandon. Some lesbians claim that Deneuve is not actually in the scene, but rather a body double is used in her place, a rumor which is often told with considerable disappointment. However, the truth of the rumor (a body double *is* intercut with shots of Deneuve) seems less important than its existence in the first place, which suggests that lesbians have spent a lot of time scrutinizing this scene on their home videotapes, giving the vampire relationship a kind of legitimacy as a viable representation of lesbianism, and acknowledging its erotic potential for women.[15]

The vampire character in *The Hunger* is not based on Carmilla, but on a second source: the legend of Countess Elisabeth Bathory of Transylvania, who lived in the seventeenth century. From most accounts, she was a sexual sadist who tortured and murdered her female servants and later progressed to local noblewomen before she was caught and brought to trial. This blight on the Hungarian aristocratic landscape was immediately hushed up by church and state, and the incriminating trial testimony was considered so shocking that it was suppressed for over a hundred years.[16]

Theda Bara in *Sin* (1915).

Catherine Deneuve plays a love song while seducing Susan Sarandon in *The Hunger*.

The Hunger: The cool Catherine Deneuve kisses the hot Susan Sarandon.

In the absence of historical fact the Hungarian imagination worked overtime to fill the void. The Bathory legend spread like wildfire through villages and towns across Eastern Europe throughout the seventeenth, eighteenth and nineteenth centuries. One of the most popular myths about her is that she murdered young virgins because she believed bathing in their blood would restore her youth.

Although this myth provides the plot of the Hammer Studio film *Countess Dracula* (Peter Sasdy, 1971), in *The Hunger* the vampire is only indirectly based on the Elisabeth Bathory legend, modernizing the icon of the irresistible aristocratic woman and her ability to keep her youth at her victims' expense. But another lesbian vampire film, *Daughters of Darkness*, relies more closely on the Bathory story.

Daughters of Darkness (Harry Kumel, Belgium 1970) has enjoyed something of a cult following, not only because it stars Delphine Seyrig but also because in many ways it tends deliberately to subvert the lesbian vampire genre. For example, instead of the male voyeur watching the lesbians make love, the lesbian vampire and her lover stand outside the window and watch the heterosexual couple. Also, the vampire, Elisabeth Bathory, is the most likable character in the film. According to the standard bisexual triangle formula discussed earlier, she would represent a threat or obstacle to the heterosexual norm that the narrative of most lesbian vampire films seeks to overcome. But here, the heterosexual norm turns out to be frighteningly abnormal and nightmarish (the man who is competing against the vampire turns out to be a closet homosexual and sadistic toward women), and the lifestyle of the lesbian vampire seems like a welcome alternative. In one scene, the vampire uses a feminist critique of male behavior toward women and of heterosexuality in general, rather than any supernatural power she has, to lure her 'victim' away from the man. Elisabeth Bathory (Delphine Seyrig) mocks Valerie's (Andrea Rau) allegiance to her husband and her claim that 'Stefan loves me, whatever you think', by answering, 'that's why he wants to make of you what every man wants of every women. A slave, a thing, an object for pleasure.'

The degree of narrative closure largely influences what meanings the lesbian vampire films can generate, and the extent to which lesbians can find alternative or oppositional meanings. In the conclusion of a typical bisexual triangle film – *Personal Best, The Bostonians* – given an even fight between a heterosexual man and a lesbian, the man will win out every time, thereby restoring the 'natural order'. Heterosexuality triumphs over homosexuality, and man triumphs over woman. The typical lesbian vampire film concludes by following this same scenario, but

A portrait of the "real-life" 17th century vampire, Countess Elisabeth Bathory.

Vampire Elisabeth Bathory (Delphine Seyrig) and her lover/accomplice in *Daughters of Darkness*.

the man must invariably kill the lesbian character in order to destroy the threat she represents. Although lesbian characters are frequently killed off in any film's conclusion (*The Fox*, *The Children's Hour*), mainstream Hollywood films do not usually allow their lesbian characters to act on sexual desire. The horror film, in contrast, has an added punishment to mete out: the lesbian vampire is killed because of her active sexuality as well as her lesbianism. Seemingly sexually 'liberated' from the restraints of Hollywood, the lesbian vampire film appears to allow for women's desire but always exacts its punishment. The theorist Raymond Bellour has written,

> The masculine subject can accept the image of woman's pleasure only on the condition that, having constructed it, he may inscribe himself within it, and thus reappropriate it even at the cost of its (or her) destruction.[17]

Linda Williams has pushed this observation further, and found that 'the titillating attention given to the expression of women's desire is directly proportional to the violence perpetrated [within the film] against women.'[18]

The lesbian vampire must lose to the mortal man in the battle for possession of the mortal woman. In such a battle scene from *The Vampire Lovers*, perfect symmetry is achieved: the scene opens with Carmilla carrying Emma down the stairs, and ends with Karl, the male victor, carrying Emma back up the stairs. Carmilla's attempt to take Emma away with her is interrupted; the scene is intercut with Karl racing up on his white horse. He enters the house, the struggle takes place, and with the help of the cross (a vampire-repellent), good triumphs over evil. Emma, like the spoils of war, has exchanged hands and the audience supposedly sighs with relief.

The typical lesbian vampire film, belonging within the horror/exploitation genre, is an articulation of men's subconscious fear of and hostility toward women's sexuality. The lesbian vampire seduction embodies myths common not only to vampirism but to women's sexuality as it traditionally has been defined in the cinema, and links the fear of vampirism with the male fear of women. The vampire's thirst for blood and the association of blood with menstruation makes mocking reference to female life-giving capacities, inverting them into life-taking ones. The lesbian vampire film uses lesbianism as titillation that is at once provocative and conquerable, and equates lesbian sexual powers with unnatural powers. It appeals to deep, dark fears of the insatiable female, the consuming mother, the devouring mother, woman as monster, the 'vagina dentata'. To the extent that seduction rather than violent coercion implies some degree of complicity, it depicts a consensual relationship between two women as inherently pathological, with the self-preservation of the one appealing to the self-destructiveness of the other. One woman's survival is always at the other's expense.

If the lesbian vampire dramatizes men's fears, anxieties, and hatred of women, is it possible for lesbians to derive pleasure from such films? The lesbian vampire is the most powerful representation of lesbianism to be found on the commercial movie screen, and rather than abandon her for what she signifies, it may be possible to extricate her from her original function, and reappropriate her power.

James Donald has argued that the vampire film does 'present the Other as a threat . . . ' but it is not limited to this function. He writes that vampire films 'are not just ideological mechanisms for domesticating terror and repression in popular culture . . . [but are] also symptoms of the instability of culture, the impossibility of its closure or perfection'.[19] In the lesbian vampire films that fall outside of the low budget horror/exploitation genre, this impossibility of cultural closure is paralleled precisely by an impossibility of narrative closure, which in turn lends itself to alternative viewing strategies by lesbian spectators. Drawing heavily on European art cinema conventions, the films *Blood and Roses*, *The Hunger* and *Daughters of Darkness* use higher production budgets, well-known actors and directors, and don't rely on violence and nudity to hold the viewer. But it is not their art-film status so much as their more ambiguous endings (which is, after all, an art cinema characteristic) which allow for a wider range of readings. In these conclusions, the vampire is still physically destroyed but the woman whom she seduced becomes a vampire herself through the transmigration of the vampire's soul. And as the lesbian vampire lives on in a new body, the cycle that is set in motion by her first appearance continues beyond the film's ending. Because of this, these films can be seen as departures from the genre, even as they draw heavily from it. Bonnie Zimmerman has suggested that *Daughters of Darkness* is open to lesbian reinterpretation because of the romantic, transhistorical appeal of the film's ending, in which the vampire's spirit 'occupies a new body once it is deprived of the old, suggesting that lesbianism is eternal, passing effortlessly from one woman to another'.[20]

Lesbians can also find erotic elements in scenes which do not feature direct displays of sexuality. This is certainly true of *Dracula's Daughter*, and perhaps *Blood and Roses* as well. In *Dracula's Daughter*, produced in 1936, the spectator's sympathy is with the vampire (Gloria Holden). With the advent of psychology as a more widely accepted field of science,

Dracula's Daughter: Gloria Holden inherits her unfortunate affliction from her father.

Gloria Holden mesmerizes her victim in *Dracula's Daughter.*

lesbianism and vampirism are presented as uncontrollable afflictions for which the tormented lesbian vampire herself seeks professional help. The Countess tries but fails to escape her family heritage of vampirism; she seduces young women before being destroyed by the doctor who failed to cure her. Gloria Holden is beautiful and the film is elegantly stylized in black and white, elements which help make the film pleasurable for contemporary (if not also historical) lesbian audiences. In *Blood and Roses* (1960), external events such as a masquerade ball and a fireworks display are used to suggest Carmilla's inner turmoil; such events are also symbols for the film's repressed lesbianism which emerges in only a few, very restrained scenes. There may be pleasure for lesbian viewers in the discovery of these subtextual lesbian scenes, and in reading them as lesbian.

While *The Vampire Lovers* uses the male vampire hunter as a stand-in for the perspective of the male spectator, *Blood and Roses* uses a similar voice-over narration device, but here it is the voice of Carmilla herself, telling her own story. This shift in the position of the narrator contributes to lesbian spectators' pleasure in the vampire's seductions; it is as though she has made a pact with the lesbian viewer which turns her into an accomplice.

Lesbian vampire films can further encourage a unique reception by lesbian spectators, because of the powerful erotic connotations of the vampire relationship and its expression of a secret and forbidden sexuality. But more commonly, certain problems of representation and spectatorship work against such a reception. The typical vampire and her victim are both visually coded as heterosexual and feminine, even though the narrative sets them up to be lovers. They lack the lesbian verisimilitude that would enable them to 'pass' as lesbians; they flirt with men and dress (and undress) to appeal to male desire. If they do not offer the same image of erotic fascination for women that they are intended to provide for heterosexual men, neither do they pose the same threat for lesbian viewers as they do for men. As a result, the lesbian spectator's relationship to the vampire takes a different form: neither sexually desirable nor sexually threatening, the lesbian vampire is appealing only for the power she wields. Instead of feeling endangered, lesbians can derive vicarious enjoyment from the vampire's dangerous powers. But due to her unique position, the lesbian spectator doesn't develop a fear of the vampire. And of course, as a horror film, it then falls flat. Without the element of danger, the film becomes a burlesque, to be appreciated primarily as camp.

Although usually considered to be the province of gay male culture, camp is a frequent component of lesbian spectatorship as well, arising from the relationship between theatrical and melodramatic qualities in the cinema on the one hand, and those perceptions of the world which are informed by one's gayness, on the other. Critic Jack Babuscio has identified four features basic to the definition of camp: irony, aestheticism, theatricality, and humor. His definition is a useful starting point for understanding the subversive strategies of camp for lesbian spectators. Certainly there is irony in the lesbian vampire film. The lesbian vampire is incongruous socially; she is not what she seems to be, and her difference is not detected by those around her despite some obvious signs. This incongruity can be especially appreciated by lesbians who often find themselves in a similar social situation.

Furthermore, camp identifies itself through artifice and aestheticism, rejecting and opposing puritan morality.[21] Since lesbian spectators can dismiss the puritan morality represented by the vampire hunters (good Christian men), they are freer to enjoy the film's exaggerated, predictable imagery and obvious theatricality, the vampire's 'masking of "abnormality" behind a facade of "normality" '.[22]

Finally, camp relies on humor. Babuscio writes, 'Camp can... be a means of undercutting rage by its derision of concentrated bitterness. Its vision of the world is comic.'[23] Camp humor is a way of exposing and disempowering those cultural myths and representations which would otherwise be unrelentingly oppressive, especially to women and gay people. Susan Sontag calls camp 'a solvent of morality [which] neutralizes moral indignation'.[24] An example of lesbian spectators' use of camp to displace immobilizing rage and indignation can be found in relation to yet another horror film whose victims are female. At a gay liberation film series in the early 1970s in New York, during a screening of *Invasion of the Body Snatchers*, a lesbian yelled out from the back of the audience, 'Save me a breast!'[25]

The dominant cinema demands that men do the looking and women are looked at. The lesbian vampire breaks through this cinematic relationship and actively looks. She remains the object of male desire but also becomes the agent for female desire – dangerous, excessive, lesbian desire. This contradiction begs the question: Can cultural myths about the 'dark side' of women's sexuality be reworked into a framework which is empowering rather than victimizing? Recent lesbian vampire films by independent filmmakers – such as Bruna Fionda, Polly Gladwin, and Isiling Mack-Nataf's *Mark of Lilith* (Great Britain, 1986) and Amy

Goldstein's highly stylized *Because the Dawn* (United States, 1988) – begin to explore this possibility. The former raises the question of where such a process of reappropriation might lead, while the latter reverses the power relation so that it is the vampire who is desired – the mortal woman stalks the streets at night in search of her. But even if such a complete 'revamping' of the genre is ultimately not possible, a camp reading provides a powerful antidote. Camp creates the space for an identification with the vampire's secret, forbidden sexuality which doesn't also demand participation in one's own victimization as a requisite for cinematic pleasure.

5

Women's 'Art' Cinema and
Its Lesbian Potential

The post-war European art cinema's courtship of lesbianism is some-
thing of a love/hate affair. Unlike Hollywood, the art cinema has
not shied away from the representation of lesbian subject matter: Roberto
Rossellini's *Rome, Open City* (Italy, 1946), Ingmar Bergman's *Persona*
(Sweden, 1965), Bernardo Bertolucci's *The Conformist* (Italy, 1970),
Rainer Werner Fassbinder's *The Bitter Tears of Petra von Kant* (W. Germany,
1972), Derek Jarman's *Jubilee* (U.K., 1973), Lina Wertmuller's *Sotto Sotto*
(Italy, 1984), Liliana Cavani's *A Berlin Affair* (Italy, 1987), and Louis
Malle's *May Fools* (France, 1990), among others, attest to a large body
of work in which lesbian imagery is not repressed or excised. On the
other hand, much of this imagery can be problematic and disturbing
for lesbian spectators, and tends to convey through images what the
Hollywood cinema conveys through absence.[1] Yet the appeal of lesbianism
for the art cinema is undeniably powerful, an appeal which is unparalleled
either by its more conventional Hollywood neighbors on the one side or by
its more experimental, avant garde neighbors (who have a rich tradition
of gay male imagery) on the other. As a form which considers sexuality a
serious matter, the art cinema has found lesbian content to be a legitimate
arena for exploration.

But the art cinema is important for lesbians in another way: for the
fact that most women directors concerned with lesbian representation
are relying on the modes of production of the art cinema, if not also
working within its filmic conventions. Although the art cinema's narrative
voice is usually aligned with male subjectivity, still it shares many stylistic
properties with women's feature filmmaking. And significantly, it is within
this European art cinema context and its precedent of state-subsidized
production motivated by other factors besides pure profit that most feature

films directed by women are able to be produced. In 1982, for example, Marlene Gorris directed her first film, *A Question of Silence*. She raised approximately one-third of the production budget, which committed the Dutch government to funding the rest, despite her lack of prior experience. Such a financial obligation by the state is astonishing to non-European filmmakers, although, regrettably, it is diminishing quickly as the European film industry becomes less concerned with maintaining national film cultures than with competing financially against Hollywood products for European box offices.

Making use of this state-subsidized art cinema production system and drawing upon the resurgence of a large feminist movement in the early 1970s, women's feature filmmaking emerged in the last two decades as a diverse body of work that only unfairly gets squeezed into a single category or genre. This diversity owes much to the emphasis on individual artistic vision, which it shares with the art cinema, and to differing historical circumstances and attitudes toward the cinema in the various countries where these films are produced.[2] What unifies women's feature filmmaking, then, is not its stylistic qualities or national origin, nor even the gender of its director, but rather its bringing together some of the visual codes of other, non-classical modes of cinema with the political and personal agendas of feminism, resulting in a new kind of film. It is this combination of seemingly disparate, relatively marginal discourses – art cinema, avant garde cinema, feminism – that both defines women's feature filmmaking and opens up the possibility for the representation of lesbian desire.

This combination is crucial, because it helps to account for that hard-to-define 'something' which distinguishes the work of many women directors from that of their male art cinema colleagues. Richard Dyer finds:

> One impact of the new feminism was a growth in the number of women who got to direct films within European art cinema, previously very much a preserve of the male *auteur*. It is striking how many of these films, though speaking from a heterosexual (or unclear) position, provide very affirmative images of lesbianism, often seen as an enviable alternative to relations between the sexes or else as part of an exploration of women bonding together, dissolving distinctions between comrades, friends, and lovers.[3]

While it is undeniably true that a large number of films that fit in that gray area between women's cinema and art cinema offer 'affirmative images' of lesbianism, many seem to do so with one hand while taking them away with the other. This throws up interesting questions: Do such films address the spectator as female, and does that address include lesbians? Do they create a space for lesbian desire to be expressed? Or do they, as much of the art cinema does, use lesbianism as titillation; do they promise but not deliver?

These questions depend on both text and context: such factors as audience expectations, cultural attitudes, and exhibition venues all play a role in the response a particular film elicits. While lesbians might well feel 'conned' if they went to see a film such as Diane Kurys's *Entre Nous* in a gay or lesbian film festival, they might be pleasantly surprised to stumble upon it at the New York Film Festival, where films focusing on female relationships are rare indeed. Because for British and American audiences these European films, as Charlotte Brunsdon has put it, 'occupy both an art cinema and a women's film space',[4] and because of the tyranny of the box office in determining film programming, many lesbians outside of major urban areas, or outside the sphere of the cultural or educational institutions which have access to these films, are simply unable to see them. As a result only a privileged minority of lesbians is familiar with even these relatively widely screened and discussed films, and distribution and exhibition practices, together with the work's proximity to the art cinema, conspire to keep it so. (A number of the films have recently been issued on videotape, although distribution remains extremely limited.)

Whether such films offer the potential for lesbian pleasure in the cinema, or instead function to close down that potential, may have less to do with the director's gender, sexuality, or conscious intentions than with the conventions of art cinema on which women's cinema so often relies. To sort this out, some definitions of the art cinema are in order.

David Bordwell in his essay, 'The Art Cinema as a Mode of Film Practice', notes that the art cinema emerged as a post-war phenomenon, as Hollywood began its slow decline in dominance, and that it possesses 'a definite historical existence, a set of formal conventions, and implicit viewing procedures'.[5] Beyond differences in narrative content – and its fascination with lesbianism – the art cinema is distinctive in its use of stylization, subjective vision, ambiguity, and loose narrative structure. In outlining the formal conventions of the art cinema, Bordwell first finds the cause and effect linkage of events in art cinema to be looser and more tenuous than that in Hollywood cinema, giving the narrative a drifting, episodic quality:

Characters may wander out and never reappear; events may lead to nothing. The Hollywood protagonist speeds directly toward the target; lacking a goal, the art-film character slides passively from one situation to another.[6]

Virtually all of Chantal Akerman's characters could be described in this way, even though her films do not fit easily and comfortably within art cinema. *Je Tu Il Elle* (Belgium, 1974) and *Les Rendez-Vous D'Anna* (Belgium, 1979) reveal events which lead to nothing and characters who wander passively from one situation to another; they also bring in a feminist concern with positioning women's experiences at the center of the narrative and with attempting to articulate lesbian desire. Akerman's films, especially these two, suggest on the one hand that art cinema has proved more useful to women feature filmmakers than other film practices, and yet on the other, that some women directors have radically critiqued and altered the meanings of art cinema's salient characteristics by bringing them together with other non-dominant film practices, such as minimalism and the avant garde, and most significantly, with feminism.

Je Tu Il Elle takes the form of a black/white triptych: three loosely connected sections which feature the same central character (Je), played by Chantal Akerman herself. In the first section, a young woman is having difficulty writing a letter; sometimes she scribbles feverishly, at other times she sits and stares, at others she compulsively eats sugar out of a paper bag. Although she is the only character on screen at this point, she is marginal rather than central: she doesn't speak (her own disembodied voice provides narration); her apartment, empty and dark, indicates her alienation from the outside world. Food, clothing, and shelter are minimal. At one point a man walks by the apartment, and his presence is a startling disruption of this closed interior space. His fleeting proximity to the door is a catalyst for her to enter the outside world; she pulls on her clothes and walks out.

Charlotte Brunsdon places Chantal Akerman firmly within the art cinema tradition:

> Chantal Akerman's monosyllabic, restless heroines are partly pleasurable because they offer a feminine figure starring in the familiar 'what is the meaning of life?' art cinema story. And, crucially, their lack of speech is within the best art cinema traditions of refusing to remove ambiguity about possible answers.[7]

While Akerman's narratives and characters share that passive, drifting quality of the art cinema, of all Akerman's films, *Je Tu Il Elle* is hardly pleasurable or familiar. In placing a woman instead of a man in the central role, the film reveals how the art cinema is no less bound by patriarchal culture than is the dominant cinema, and this cannot be redressed by merely substituting one gender with another. 'Je', a nameless woman, is at the center of the narrative, and yet she remains extremely marginal, raising the question of whether it is even possible to create a non-masculine 'Je' and a non-patriarchal place of authority from which to speak. Her inability to speak or write carries none of the authority that the art cinema has imparted to its male protagonists; her silence also problematizes the attempt to articulate her desire for another woman, which we later learn is the objective of the letter she fails to write, and also the objective of this first section of the film.

There is an ironic footnote to this discussion which further points to the perils of patriarchal language. In *Je Tu Il Elle* both 'Je' and 'Tu' are female. 'Je' clearly is – we see the character (played by Akerman) on screen – but 'tu' is more ambiguous. 'Tu' may refer to the spectator, but it also refers to the addressee of the letter which is never written or sent, who we later learn is a woman. The English subtitles, however, indicate that the recipient is a man; if 'je' is feminized and 'tu' is her lover, the translator's assumption is that 'tu' must be masculine.[8] When this same character is referred to in the third person, the English translation gives us 'he'. Thus, Amy Taubin, reviewing the film in the *Village Voice*, can say: 'She's writing and rewriting a letter to a man (a lover?) whose rejection seems to have precipitated her rejection and withdrawal.'[9] This mistranslated pronoun can render the scant narrative unintelligible (disconnecting the letter writing in the first section from the visit to the girlfriend in the third section), while indicating the heterosexual assumptions of language even within a feminist text.

The woman walks into the night, beginning the second section. Near the highway a truck-driver (Niels Arestrup) stops his truck and picks her up; her marginality expressed in the apartment now takes the form of silent, dispassionate observing. She watches him and listens to his stories about his wife; she is a passive listener. In the truckstop they watch a mindless TV program on the wall; she is a passive viewer. Back in the truck, she gives the driver a handjob. In this scene Akerman stridently disobeys the art cinema's rules governing the use of the female body (and especially the lesbian body) for men's visual pleasure – rules which equate Woman with sexuality and justify her heightened eroticism on the basis of 'art'. Here the woman is positioned completely off-screen, and within the frame we are only shown the truck-driver behind the wheel, driving and giving her instructions. Not the object of male desire, she is also not an agent of female desire; she moves through the scene passively, with little will of her own.

In the third section, she has arrived at the apartment of her girlfriend (Claire Wauthion). After some extreme awkwardness, she eats. In fact, she is ravenous. Her needs, first for food and then for sex, take her out of the passive, observer role; she now becomes childlike, vulnerable, demanding, active. Finally they go into the bedroom to make love. Amy Taubin writes, 'In her boisterous passion, Akerman is no longer the observer, and we are cast out, separated from her, uncomfortable in our solitary, and public, voyeurism.'[10] In other words, it is at the sex scene that our identification with the character breaks down.

This breakdown of identification probably occurs differently for different spectators according to their sexual orientation. The feeling of being left out described by Taubin may account for the discomfort some (if not most) heterosexual viewers experience, but for lesbians it may have more to do with problems of visually representing lesbian passion in a non-voyeuristic way than with the discomfort of being a voyeur. The lovemaking scene is carefully constructed against cinematic traditions and audience expectations, resisting voyeurism and fetishism through formal elements. The camera is positioned to create medium shots at a low angle. The few relatively close-up shots, rather than invading or fragmenting the women's bodies, reveal the tops of their heads, disrupting the scene by confusing the image and protecting it from our scrutiny. The soundtrack, which features quite a bit of thrashing about on the bed, undercuts the scene's potential as spectacle by its disturbingly loud volume. Janet Maslin, reviewing the film in the *New York Times*, found the scene devoid of eroticism; she describes it as an athletic tussle.[11] On the other hand, Pamela Pratt in the *New York Native*, a gay newspaper, found it erotic because of its rejection of eroticism: ' . . . bodies stick together with sweat, limbs get in the way. It is beautiful, every breathless, awkward moment of it.'[12]

This possibly erotic but absolutely uneroticized lesbian lovemaking scene must be credited for its courage in 1974, especially given that it includes the filmmaker in the scene and rejects art cinema conventions governing lesbian sexuality. The filmmaker's participation contributes directly to the scene's anti-aestheticism: Akerman herself claimed that 'I always wanted to play the part myself. I tried using someone else but it was too aesthetic.'[13] The roughness and explicitness of the scene stand in stark contradiction to the art cinema's heightened, glamorized eroticism of the female figure. As Mandy Merck has argued,

> ... If lesbianism hadn't already existed, art cinema might have invented it. To a cinema which affects an attitude of high seriousness in matters sexual, the lesbian romance affords a double benefit. It provides a sufficient degree of difference from dominant cinematic representations of sex and sexuality ... yet it does this by offering – quite literally – more of the same (the same being that old cinema equation 'woman=sexuality' which the art cinema, despite its differences with Hollywood, has rarely forsaken).[14]

The discomfort that some lesbian spectators experience watching the uneroticized love scene in *Je Tu Il Elle* may be symptomatic of the problems in attempting to reject these omnipresent masculine conventions of sexual representation without also totally rejecting sexually charged content and images.

Akerman's *Les Rendez-Vous D'Anna* fits more securely within the art cinema model, softening the avant garde tendencies of *Je Tu Il Elle*. *Les Rendez-Vous D'Anna*, like *Je Tu Il Elle*, fulfills Bordwell's first characteristic of the art cinema in its loose, random narrative structure: its protagonist, Anna (Aurore Clement), goes from one town and one episode to another. We see her in train stations, phone booths, hotel rooms, alone and with several men. Anna's wandering is justified in the film by her profession (she is a successful filmmaker showing her work), but it functions more strongly as an expression of her lack of fulfillment (despite her success). This disillusionment with success is certainly in keeping with the art cinema's search for the meaning of life, and this use of character subjectivity to structure the narrative is another common art cinema ploy.

Furthermore, continuing with Bordwell's outline of art cinema practises, the author/director 'becomes a formal component, the overriding intelligence organizing the film for our comprehension ... Lacking identifiable stars and familiar genres, the art cinema uses a concept of authorship to unify the text.'[15] In *Les Rendez-Vous D'Anna* Chantal Akerman not only continues those certain stylistic signatures which identify her films as 'Chantal Akerman films' – real-time durations, avoidance of close-up shots, long steady camera holds, symmetrical frame compositions – but also inscribes herself within the film text through the central figure of a woman filmmaker.

In the first shot of the film, a shot which incorporates all of these stylistic signatures, Anna goes into a phone booth on the train platform

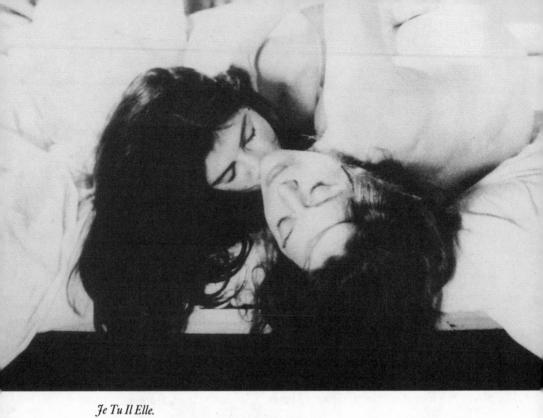

Je Tu Il Elle.

Anna and her mother in *Les Rendez-Vous D'Anna.*

to make a call, but no one seems to answer. She places the call again once she is in her hotel room, again without success. Like the unsuccessful letter in *Je Tu Il Elle*, the phone call is a frustrated attempt to reach her female lover. We learn this in a later scene, in what must be the most bizarre 'coming out' story ever filmed. In a hotel room with her mother, Anna tells of her affair with a woman. She recounts how it began: 'She came to see me . . . We lay down on the bed and kept talking. Our bodies happened to touch. Suddenly we were kissing. I don't know how it happened. I felt nauseous . . . I let myself go. It felt good.' Then, back to the present, 'Shall we go to bed? Aren't you going to undress?' In the end of the scene, Anna is naked, in bed, embracing her mother.

Because *Les Rendez-Vous D'Anna* follows the art cinema conventions more closely than *Je Tu Il Elle* (and in fact more closely than any of Akerman's previous films), it more clearly subscribes to certain specific viewing strategies which the art cinema demands – strategies which determine how we are encouraged to view this peculiar scene. The art cinema relies on a loose cause/effect narrative because it is motivated more by psychological causation than by actions. Characters frequently tell stories which explain their psychological states; in *Les Rendez-Vous D'Anna*, the scene described above serves this purpose.

On the one hand, this recounting of the awkward beginning of an off-screen love affair with a woman contrasts with and begins to explain Anna's rather meaningless on-screen sexual encounters with men. Anna goes through empty gestures with men, but has unrealizable desire for a woman she cannot even reach on the telephone. If this story illuminates her psychological state, and her psychological state motivates the narrative (according to art cinema conventions), then her misdirected desire is the source of her unfulfillment in life, which is expressed through her aimless travelling. But the visual displacement of the lover by the mother in the scene takes this meaning further, imposing onto the articulation of lesbianism a visual enactment of a pre-Oedipal, narcissistic identification between mother and daughter, replete with the mother's demand to 'let me look at you awhile' and warnings not to tell her father about the lesbian affair. This scene could possibly be read as an ironic critique of the psychological construction of sexual identity, but the formal and narrative structures of the film complicate such a reading. It is difficult to view the visual image as an ironic critique of what is at the same time being conveyed verbally as 'explanation' of the character's psychological state. In several screenings of the film with feminist audiences, the predominant response to this scene was unexplained feelings of discomfort and despair.[16] Even if we allow for an ironic reading, the scene still keeps us locked within a psychological 'explanation' for lesbian desire that is grossly inadequate.

In the film's final scene, a loose resolution is provided in the form of a message from the lover on Anna's phone machine, paralleling the attempted call that began the narrative. But the closure is empty, unfulfilled. Richard Kwietniowsky has called *Les Rendez-Vous D'Anna* 'the antithesis of the traditional "love story" ': Anna is silent when she is with men who make demands of her, but consistently tries to speak to her female lover; meanwhile, her female lover remains unseen throughout the film and silent until the final shot.[17] Akerman dismantles both heterosexual romantic myths and the structures for male visual pleasure, but she cannot envisage any alternative film language for female desire.

There is a moment in another film, Marlene Gorris's *A Question of Silence* (Netherlands, 1982), which seems to correspond to the 'coming out' scene in *Les Rendez-Vous D'Anna*. This moment also introduces the possibility of lesbianism and then retreats from it, while shedding light on otherwise inexplicable tensions underlying the narrative. Gorris's treatment of lesbianism can be seen as an inversion of Akerman's: whereas Akerman de-eroticizes a sexual scene in *Je Tu Il Elle*, Gorris eroticizes a non-sexual scene; whereas Akerman uses a spoken story about desire for an unseen woman in *Les Rendez-Vous D'Anna*, Gorris's lesbian scene is silent and told visually.

Of course *A Question of Silence* cannot really be compared with *Les Rendez-Vous D'Anna*; they differ fundamentally in the use of characters and dialogue, in narrative structure, in *mise en scène*, camera style and so on. Gorris originally approached Akerman with the screenplay for *A Question of Silence*, but Akerman encouraged Gorris to direct it herself, thus launching Gorris's directorial career. The result is a more formally conventional film, with higher production values and the visual style of mainstream European art-house movies. But there is a point at which Gorris's and Akerman's work connects: both directors rely on certain art cinema conventions yet put them to feminist purposes. They also both approach and avoid the problems of lesbian representation, a process which opens up, only to then close down, the potential for lesbian visual pleasure.

In the 'lesbian' scene within *A Question of Silence*, a psychiatrist and her client stand in close proximity, facing each other in the client's prison cell. The client holds her hands several inches away from the psychiatrist and moves them slowly to outline her body. The women do not touch or speak, and the scene is interrupted when a man enters the room, suggesting both the possibility and impossibility of lesbianism.[18] The medium shot places us, the viewers, in a similar proximity to the women as they are to each other. We see them from the waist up, viewing as much of their bodies as they would clearly see of each other. Although we see them from the side, they are face to face. This refusal to use point of view shots to align our identification with a particular character and the simultaneous closeness to and distance from the image implicates the viewer in the lesbian dynamic. The viewer participates not through recognizing a specific lesbian character, of whom there is none, but in lesbianism as a way of being and understanding each other that involves both intimacy and boundaries, that respects both the connections and the spaces between women.

The differences between the two women are maintained in this scene, rendered narratively: between the psychiatrist's marital and class privilege and role as doctor, and her client's position as worker (secretary), prisoner, and patient. Still, the power relation, inherent in these differences, is mitigated by several factors: a connection through gender, the fact that it is the client who initiates the interaction, and a shared knowledge not through spoken language but through the female body.

Although this one scene makes the film's only direct reference to lesbianism, it is not an isolated moment of lesbian potential unfulfilled, buried in an otherwise heterosexual narrative. Despite the lack of lesbian characters or events, the film is premised on an underlying woman-centered ideology which surfaces in this and other, non-lesbian scenes, As such, lesbianism is not an individual psychological problem but is positioned within a female continuum which privileges relationships between women over those with men.

The plot of the film, told through flashbacks, focuses on three 'ordinary' women – a middle-aged waitress (Nelly Frijda), a perceptive, articulate secretary (Henriette Tol), and a young mother/housewife stifled by the confinement of her role (Edda Barends). Strangers to each other, they find themselves in the same boutique one fine day and mercilessly kill the shop-owner. The court appoints a female psychiatrist, who tries to determine the sanity of the murderers, and who must make her own personal odyssey in order to do so. Her quest forces her to examine her assumptions about men and women, and ultimately to re-evaluate her own life. Although she begins with an attitude of smugness and elitism, it is soon obvious that she has much to learn from these less privileged women who are locked up in jail for murder. Increasingly estranged from her husband, the psychiatrist momentarily puts aside the analytic tools of her trade and, with sudden clarity, speaks to him from another kind of knowledge (which he can't understand): 'Haven't you seen photos of war atrocities?'

The narrative of the film is structured so that we are to identify with this personal odyssey of the psychiatrist, which Charlotte Brunsdon characterizes as being 'from non-feminist heterosexuality to woman-identification'.[19] The psychiatrist's point of departure is an 'enlightened' middle class marriage to an 'enlightened' man, who cooks, permits her to juggle a career and wifehood, and even occasionally lets her initiate sex (as she does in the film's opening scene). In the *New York Times*, Janet Maslin describes the journey like this: 'The psychiatrist, who is first shown to be very happy with her husband, grows to hate him during the course of the story, and finds herself attracted to the most bold and outspoken of her patients.'[20] But the film is not the 'coming out' story Maslin suggests; the lesbian quality to the film does not relate to the sexual identity of a particular character but rather to a way of making sense of the connections between women in general. In the course of the film the psychiatrist discovers a wellspring of deeply hidden female rage, a rage that could erupt into murder, and this discovery leads her to understand that, despite obvious differences, there is a shared undercurrent between her life and the lives of other women. Here we have a reversal of the usual art cinema progression: rather than relying on psychological motivation to understand the three murderers, the psychiatrist (and by extension, the spectator) comes to understand them by rejecting psychological tools. A somewhat utopian shared female value system replaces traditional male logic as the organizing principle of the film.

The film's momentum builds toward the trial scene and the psychiatrist's startling declaration that the women are sane. The male judge and lawyer are not caricatures; they are average men trying but failing to comprehend the crime. The power of justice is in their clumsy hands, in contrast to the more evocative, unnamed power of the women in the courtroom. These women – the defendants, the psychiatrist, the courtroom audience of women who were witnesses to the crime but never came forward – suddenly erupt into uncontrollable laughter, a laughter that none of the men can understand. B. Ruby Rich, reviewing the film in the *Village Voice*, writes:

> ... it is precisely this laughter which forges a bond among wom-. en, and between women viewers and the film, for this transgressive

laughter – that overflows its boundaries and manifests itself to excess – is intimately connected to its flip side, the rage that does the same.[21]

As Rich argues, the film can be empowering for female spectators, but it should also be pointed out that it loses many along the way. On the level of narrative, as I've stated, the film's structure allows the audience to identify with the psychiatrist and follow her transition in order to come to a similar understanding. It is a good ploy, urging liberal spectators into a more radical position. But liberal feminists have often found the violence of the murder too horrific to support, and refuted what they read as the film's advocacy of violence against men as the solution to women's oppression. Liberal critics, male and female, almost unanimously interpreted the film's understanding of female rage as an endorsement of murder, and wrote that 'the feminist cause will not be well served by *A Question of Silence*', calling the film 'a shocking perversion of [feminism]', 'excessive in its presentation of the female cause', 'the unacceptable face of feminism'.[22] Heterosexual women who could accept the murder on the level of metaphor most likely lost the film at the point where heterosexuality is linked with marital rape (the psychiatrist's husband turns out not to be that enlightened), and the film moves quickly toward a female separatist position. In screenings at New York City's Waverly Theater, the men in the audience seemed to be visibly threatened by violence aimed at men by women instead of the other way around, and by the replacement of male logic with female rage. Shifting around uncomfortably in his seat, virtually each man in the room put his arm around 'his' woman next to him, physically asserting his challenged authority. If the film alienated most of the men and a good proportion of the women who went to see it, who already, because of its subtitles, its art-house location, and its tag as 'feminist', were a select group of the filmgoing public, for whom did it 'work'?

Marlene Gorris claims that her film does not intentionally address women:

> I'm not making film for a specific audience. Neither film [*A Question of Silence* nor her subsequent feature, *Broken Mirrors*] is seen mainly by women. It's seen by men as well. I make those films because I'm interested in the ways of the world, as far as the power struggle goes.[23]

Such a statement should make one wary of relying on the filmmaker's intention as the sole determining factor in how certain films elicit certain responses. Although the narrative of the film intentionally encourages an identification with the character of the psychiatrist, other factors work against such an identification. Jeanette Murphy has observed how the film uses few close-ups, maintains a respectful distance and avoids point of view shots, all of which prevent the kind of passive, absorbing identification associated with most mainstream films.[24] Because the film does not demand this kind of traditional character identification, lesbian spectators can find something else with which to identify – the connections between women – and because of this one could say the film is structured, intentionally or not, to address lesbians. But given its feminist assumptions and the whiteness of its cast, this address might well be limited to white, predominantly middle class lesbian-feminists.

Even this could be further qualified, to white, predominantly middle class lesbian-feminists of a certain era. *A Question of Silence* is the product of and speaks to a particular moment in Western feminism, a moment which is passing or perhaps has already passed. The utopian connections between women that it establishes can only be understood within the passion of the 1970s radical feminist politics which sees women's subjugation at the heart of all other oppression, and which sees woman as a fundamentally different animal from man, a position which has been on the decline over the 1980s. Theories of historical and cultural constructions of gender (as opposed to femaleness or maleness as a biological 'essence'), and the influence women of color have exerted on feminist thought have shifted the focus of feminist discourse away from celebrations of commonality among women to an exploration of diversity and difference. The changes in feminist thought over the past decade have combined to make the position of *A Question of Silence* seem somewhat quaint and old-fashioned in the 1990s rather than politically urgent and volatile.

But for those lesbians for whom the film worked in the 1980s, and for those for whom it still works now, it works completely. Rather than identifying with the psychiatrist or any other character, lesbians tend to identify with the interactions between the characters, with the fantasy of women's connections to each other which, in a heterosexual scenario (feminist or not) invariably get diffused by women's connections to men. Without representing a lesbian character or lesbian sexuality and experience, *A Question of Silence* offers the possibility of lesbianism not only as an 'alternative lifestyle' but as its own logical conclusion. It is an example of how a film without a lesbian character or theme can specifically address (at least some) lesbian spectators, in contrast to the many art-house films which more directly suggest or utilize lesbian themes without addressing lesbian spectators, or which in fact deny lesbian experience.

This more common approach to 'lesbian' themes can be found in such traditional art-house films as Bernardo Bertolucci's *The Conformist* (Italy, 1970). *The Conformist* uses the lesbianism of Anna Quadri (Dominique Sanda) and the wonderfully erotic tango she dances with Marcello's wife (Stefania Sandrelli) in order to fascinate and attract Marcello (Jean Louis Trintignant), and by extension the male voyeur in the audience. It is possible for lesbians to appreciate the eroticism and yet feel cheated by how it is used, especially as the film also encourages a reading in which Marcello's sympathy for fascism originates in his repressed homosexuality.

But the appropriation of lesbian content or characters while excluding lesbian spectators holds true for 'feminist' films as well. Jill Godmillow's *Waiting for the Moon* (U.S.A., 1987), an American independent feature, combines its reliance on the formal conventions of the European art cinema with the traditional Hollywood erasure of lesbian experience. In her film, the most famous lesbians in history, Gertrude Stein and Alice B. Toklas, become asexual because, as Godmillow insists, 'If they'd been a man and a woman, we wouldn't need a bedroom scene to prove they were a couple. I refused to make that extra gesture simply because they were lesbians.'[25] But two women in bed together is not the only possible way to represent lesbian desire or a lesbian relationship; the film could have offered, but steadfastly refuses, a gesture, phrase, or exchange of looks which might be read as lesbian. Godmillow provides extra-textual material, in the form of production notes, to help the viewer (in typical art cinema fashion) understand the filmmaker's authorial intentions and to confirm the film's realism. She sets out to educate her less informed spectators of 'what in *Waiting for the Moon* is fact, and what is just plain poetic license'. In this list, however, she neglects to mention what in the lives of Gertrude and Alice was a central fact, and how it is omitted from the film as poetic license.[26] The film attracts lesbian spectators to the box office on the basis of its subject (and was actually shown in several gay and lesbian film festivals), only to result in disappointment and betrayal.

A more ambiguous example, and more successful film, is Diane Kurys's *Entre Nous* (France, 1984), released in Great Britain as *Coup de Foudre*. *Entre Nous* occupies more of a traditional art cinema space than a feminist one: it premiered in the New York Film Festival, was released by United Artists Classics, and stars major French actresses Miou Miou and Isabelle Huppert. Furthermore, it emphasizes the director as 'auteur' by presenting itself as virtually autobiographical, the story of the director's mother as perceived by the daughter. Jane Root

A silent, intimate encounter between the secretary and her court-appointed psychiatrist in Marlene Gorris's *A Question of Silence*.

No signs of passion between Gertrude and Alice in Jill Godmillow's *Waiting for the Moon*.

claims that its commercial success was based on 'disguising its particularly female pleasures under a cloak of art cinema respectability'.[27] Although directed by a woman and focusing on the intense friendship between two women, the film's formal qualities – so dependent are they on the codes of art cinema – restrain the women's relationship as the narrative seeks to extend it. Mandy Merck writes that the film upholds the voyeuristic approach to femininity as spectacle: for example, we watch the female protagonists, backs to the camera, compare their breasts in the mirror; the narrative inscribes public displays of women through fashion shows. Merck claims that 'It is this legitimation of the feminine spectacle which makes lesbianism such a gift to art cinema.'[28] On the other hand, this reliance on feminine spectacle for male visual pleasure does not automatically preclude lesbian visual pleasure as well, especially since other factors come into play. The film's detailed attention to the domestic and private domain of women in the 1950s – keeping the children from fighting, keeping the seams in their nylons straight – offers pleasure for women spectators in its inversion of the traditional hierarchy of cinematic images, while the shroud of ambiguity surrounding the exact nature of the women's relationship leaves space for the lesbian imagination.

Lea Pool's film, *Anne Trister* (French Canada, 1986), is also situated firmly within the art cinema practice, and here too it is the female characters who are central. The film concerns a young woman's psychological drama and relies on standard art cinema techniques: long takes, slow dissolves, symbolic settings, a dramatic jazz score which underlines (or overloads?) emotional tensions. In keeping with the art cinema's emphasis on psychological motivation, Anne Trister (Albane Guilhe) begins a search for self-understanding, catalyzed by her father's death. In a sense this search is two-fold: a search for Jewish identity through her father, and a search for sexual identity through her mother. Anne is also an artist, and the transformation of her *atelier* from warehouse to architectural environment, by far the most interesting development in the film, seems closely tied to both of these searches. The atelier was given to her by Simon, a Jewish cafe owner who was a close friend of her father's; the murals she paints there begin to resemble sand in the desert of Israel in which her father is buried early on in the film and to which she will return at the film's close.

Mary Alemany-Galway, reviewing the film in *Cinema Canada*, finds that '*Anne Trister* can be seen as a reworking of the Oedipus myth in feminist terms.'[29] In the female Oedipal scenario, the girl's transference of eroticism to the father requires a rejection of female solidarity and an acceptance of second-class status. Alemany-Galway argues that *Anne Trister* successfully shifts these terms to restore the primary relationship to the mother (through Anne's love for another woman, Alix). With insight she points out that the film's opening scene, in which Anne is lying on a bed crying while her mother watches but does not comfort her, is echoed much later in the film, but with a major difference: 'Towards the end, the scene . . . is repeated with Alix in her mother's place, but this time the mother figure crosses the space between them and holds her. This is the climax of the film.'[30]

It is surprising to read that this scene is supposedly the film's climax, even though, if this were a conventional romance, the narrative tensions between the heterosexual characters do usually build to a climax. The art cinema, with its liberal attitude toward sexual matters, would have us simply substitute the gender of one of the characters so that the film's climax could stay where it 'belongs', with the two characters finally uniting as lovers. But while the scene has Alix (Louise Marleau) joining Anne on the bed and embracing her, it is more easily read as the symbolic offering of the long withheld love of the mother than as the union of lovers. Such a reading is based not on the scene itself, with its sexual overtones, but on how the film has prepared us for it.

Early in the film the mother says, 'She never got the love she needed from me. Now it is too late.' One feels that Anne has gone out looking for this mother love, and found it in Alix. Scenes of the relationship between Alix and Anne are rather heavy-handedly intercut with scenes of Alix at work: she is a psychiatrist working closely with a young, troubled girl named Sarah. This emphatic editing serves to place Alix clearly in the role of symbolic mother in both relationships. Although the film is ostensibly a love story between two women, this association of Alix with the mother, along with other factors, works to resist or at least obscure the lesbian plot.

An additional factor is the visual representation of Anne. Although she is depicted as a Jewish beauty, there is only one scene in which she is presented in an overtly sexual way. Anne is relaxing in the bathtub when the phone rings and Alix calls her to it. We watch Anne slowly rise from the tub, and make her way through the apartment to the phone as she pulls a towel around her waist. Her movements are intended to look casual, but they retain a self-consciousness that makes the spectator suddenly very aware of her body. The call is from her old lover Pierre; it is as though her sexuality is not autonomous but gains its meaning from Pierre's desire for her, from being desired. In this way she becomes sexualized for the

Upholding the spectacle of femininity in Diane Kurys's *Entre Nous*.

Lea Pool's *Anne Trister*: Anne attempts an intimacy with Alex (left), but is rebuffed.

spectator only when called back into a heterosexual dynamic.

At one point Alix explains to Anne that, 'I like you a lot. I feel good when we're together. But . . . I'm not ready for this. I never will be.' The scene is conventionally constructed, using close-ups and shot-countershot editing, so that the two women are never together in the frame, reinforcing the rejection of lesbianism in the dialogue and underscoring the impossibility of the two women being together. This impossibility is also symbolized within the atelier. Anne has slowly developed the space itself into a work of art, in which it is impossible to discern her painted shadows and shafts of light from real windows and sunlight. In one of the film's most outstanding scenes, a bird, trapped in the atelier, flies and crashes into the painted windows, suggesting her trapped desire which can never be realized within the confines of the film.

Laura Mulvey has argued that feminist cinema must negate the Hollywood visual system of pleasure which depends on the image of woman as spectacle for the controlling male gaze. Although the art cinema has defined itself in terms of its difference from – and its own negation of – the Hollywood model, many of Hollywood's conventions regarding the representation of women remain intact or are in fact strengthened. A reliance on art cinema conventions by feminist filmmakers therefore seems to put them at cross purposes.

Some feminist filmmakers, such as Chantal Akerman and Yvonne Rainer, have avoided this trap by radically transforming art cinema practices and employing formal elements which work against voyeurism and fetishism. Yvonne Rainer's recent experimental film, *Privilege* (U.S., 1990), both resists and exposes the voyeuristic appeal of lesbianism: an erotic spoken text (from Joan Nestle's *A Restricted Country*) is delivered by the film's lesbian character, Brenda (Blaire Baron), to an audience consisting of her male lawyer and a group of people watching as if in a theater rehearsal. As the verbal story reveals an increasingly graphic tale of lesbian sex, its incongruous, absolutely non-sexual visual presentation and its allusions to performance criticize the spectacle potential of most lesbian representation. But far more frequently, feminist directors have worked closely within the traditional art cinema, bringing to it their feminist concerns of women's daily lives and relationships, and merely avoiding potentially exploitative or voyeuristic scenes.

Ulrike Ottinger's films, in contrast, reject or parody the conventions of art cinema and search for new ways to construct visual pleasure, creating various spectator positions usually neglected or marginalized by cinematic address.[31] But while she uses complex strategies of identification which appeal especially to women, she upholds, even exaggerates, the female body as spectacle. It is this which makes her work difficult to address with academic feminist theory, while it strongly appeals to female, and specifically lesbian, spectators.

Ottinger's films intersect with several non-classical cinema practices, including art cinema, surrealism, and ethnographic cinema.[32] She works in documentary as well as fiction, and her films combine, or at times juxtapose, formal strategies from both genres. Originally a painter, Ottinger is more closely connected to fantasy and surrealist film traditions than to the European art cinema – specifically New German Cinema which began in Oberhausen in 1962 – the context in which Ottinger, because of her nationality, is usually placed. According to Brunsdon, ' . . . The complex of state funding and subsidy introduced since 1964 has been organised around the concept of the "Autorenfilm" [in West Germany], . . . where there is an historically identifiable art cinema.'[33] Ottinger's work clearly belongs within the 'Autoren' school, which privileges the director's role as sole author/artist, and which extends as well to the avant garde or underground film work being made in West Germany in the 1960s and 70s. It would be wrong, based on their 'Autoren' emphasis, to situate her films within West Germany's specific brand of art cinema, New German Cinema, with its realistic, naturalistic qualities. In Ottinger's work a rejection of art cinema conventions can be found, such as its cause/effect narrative structure, its obsession with realism, and its high seriousness about sexual matters. She opts instead for a more associative visual style based on fantasy and collage, and a playfulness toward sexuality and power dynamics.

This manifests itself strongly in her 'pirate movie', *Madame X: An Absolute Ruler* (W. Germany, 1977) which, although rarely screened, has become something of a lesbian cult classic. Tossing caution to the wind, the film foils audience expectations of narrative congruity, instead drawing in its spectators on the strength of its provocative, lush imagery and the appeal of its fantasy. Madame X, from her ship the Chinese Orlando, sends out a telegram to women in all walks of life, asking them to give up their safe but boring existences in order to live the life of pirates:

Chinese Orlando – stop – to all women – stop – offer world – stop – full of gold – stop – love – stop – adventure at sea – stop – call Chinese Orlando – stop!

Rather than abandon the territory of sexuality because of the dangers it holds for women (as many women working within the art cinema have done), *Madame X* forges ahead into and transforms that territory, first of all by rejecting the seriousness with which sexuality is so often laden. In the love scene between Madame X and Noa-Noa (one of her recruits), traditional romance is parodied through exaggerated role-playing, ridiculous costumes, and a soundtrack of animal roars (and eventual purrs). The film dramatizes sexuality through rituals of power, but it does so with a strong sense of irony which is lacking in later, more conventionally art cinema lesbian films, such as Monika Treut and Elfi Mikesch's *Seduction, the Cruel Woman* (W. Germany, 1985).

Unlike the typical art cinema narrative which is propelled by uncovering the psychological motivation of the character's inner self, the characters in *Madame X* are stereotypes and stylized cliches: European artist Josephine de Collage; American housewife Betty Brillo; forest ranger Flora Tannenbaum, and so on. Although we are given a flashback sequence which 'explains' why Madame X became a pirate (her lover Orlando, played by Ottinger, was killed by a man-eating plant she was trying to present as a gift to Madame X), this explanation sheds no light on Madame X's impenetrable personality. In *Madame X* the self is anything but whole, unitary, readily available to psychological exploration. Rather it is often split, fractured or incomplete, exemplified by Madame X's 'castrated' arm (dismembered in the plant incident and embellished by a black, studded leather glove), and by Ottinger's frequent use of the 'double', in this film taking the form of the ship's figurehead, a mechanical replica of Madame X.[34]

Furthermore, the characters fluctuate and change throughout the film; their identities go through upheavals upon joining the pirate ship, living on it, dying, and returning. The androgynous figure of Bellcampo, who is rescued by the Chinese Orlando after she/he was thrown overboard a luxury yacht, embodies the ever-changing, unfixed nature of identity – as do the allusions to Orlando. Teresa de Lauretis contrasts Ottinger with Fassbinder, finding in his work a reliance on the image of Woman – fixed, mythic, symbolic – whereas in hers women retain their cultural and individual specificity.[35] Another gender contrast between the two filmmakers can also be made, however: Fassbinder's women can best be understood as men (as Ottinger herself has hinted), whereas in Ottinger's work, women are definitely women, and often, as the character of Bellcampo suggests, men are also women. But as the psychological test given to Bellcampo by the pirate ship's resident psychologist, Karla Freud Goldman, indicates, both categories are social constructions that belie uncategorizable lived experience.[36]

While a standard ploy of the art cinema is the use of a monologue to explain a character's psychological state, *Madame X* turns this attempt at scientific explanation into cliche. Karla Freud Goldman writes, and reads aloud, a letter which parodies this monologue strategy:

> During a long cruise on the Orlando my detailed observations have produced an analysis which my conscience obliges me to publish. These women, having left behind all psycho-social barriers of their daily lives, were prey to a hitherto repressed sexuality which now manifested itself with unsuspected force. Suppressed drives broke out and precipitated these women, used to the straight-jacket of civilization, into very serious psychological conflicts which crushed their weak egos. The age-old oppression of Woman which had consolidated the habits of passivity and dependence in their character structure made them docile tools in the hands of Madame X, a charismatic personality consumed with narcissism and whose lust for power grew with the quasi-masochistic submission of women beyond all bounds . . .

Since we as spectators cannot so easily unlock the characters' personalities – in fact the film, using stereotypes and role-playing, works against our doing so – we are liberated from the viewing strategies demanded by traditional art cinema. These viewing strategies are premised on a male spectatorial position: heightened psychological and sexual voyeurism, reliance on the female body to signal sexuality, and identification with the angst-ridden or alienated central male character – a process from which women are usually excluded.

It could be said that *Madame X* does rely on the female body to signal sexuality, but here it turns inside out the ways in which the art cinema (and Hollywood) have invariably represented women. In Ottinger's film the female body is undomesticated; it becomes provocative and outrageous when reinscribed in excess. Using 'traditional cinema's cliches for my own purposes',[37] Ottinger offers two characters who exaggeratedly represent 'cultural' and 'natural' sexuality: Miss Blow-Up as media-image *femme fatale*, and Noa-Noa as exotic primitive. But her use of the female body is active and aggressive; rather than place these images in passive relation to a male gaze or figure, she transgressively creates a romance *between* them.

One might argue that the women in *Madame X* also function as spectacle; Claudia Lenssen has complained that in this film,

> we find so much that is characteristic of the male avant garde:

the fetishization of beauty in the female body; the directorial concept projected onto the 'star'; images of sado-masochism . . . I was exceedingly bored by all the familiar conventions regarding female beauty; at the same time the aestheticism fascinated, even seduced me.[38]

What is curious about this statement is the conflict it reveals between the spectator's feminist political agenda and her emotional response to the film's imagery. Yet Lenssen fails to see how the aestheticism which fascinates and seduces her also works to subvert the traditional conventions which bore her. For example, the elaborately costumed, highly stylized images border on caricature, parodying traditional feminine ideals so as to uphold the spectacle quality yet destroy the illusion of realism upon which traditional cinematic spectacles, both of Hollywood and the art cinema, so often depend. In this sense they offer an exaggerated, camp quality that can have resonance for gay and, given the focus on female fantasy, especially lesbian spectators. It is this double use of spectacle, of a highly stylized, eroticized female image (such as that of Madame X herself) which also holds within it its own self-conscious parody, which contributes to the specific pleasure that women and other marginalized viewers can derive from the film.

Ottinger's recent epic, *Johanna D'Arc of Mongolia* (W. Germany, 1989) can be thought of as the fulfillment of the promise offered but not delivered by *Madame X*. *Johanna D'Arc of Mongolia* is a much more accomplished film, reflecting higher production values, years of research, and Ottinger's considerable development as a visual artist. In a sense, *Johanna D'Arc* can be seen as a continuation, twelve years later, of Ottinger's concerns already evidenced in *Madame X*: female utopian adventure stories, a fascination with China and 'Orientalism', high stylization which both dazzles the spectator and places her (or him) at an increased distance from the image. Both films feature a diverse group of women removed from their familiar cultural surroundings: in *Madame X* the pirates are women who have left their mundane lives in the patriarchy to enter a world promising them gold, love, adventure; in *Johanna D'Arc of Mongolia* the women embark on a trans-Mongolian railway journey, and find themselves kidnapped by a Mongolian princess and her band of Amazon horsewomen. Both films seduce women into leaving behind what they already know and entering into an exotic world of adventure that turns out not to be what it seems: in *Madame X* the rituals of power and domination of the patriarchy reassert themselves within the female utopia; in *Johanna D'Arc of Mongolia* the western women are made strange and exotic, and the Mongolians share the fascination of encountering the 'Other'. Most of all, both films succeed in doing something which is virtual heresy in cinematic history: they carve out a space for female fantasy, not the confined heterosexual romance fantasy of Hollywood's 'women's films', but an expansive, subversive fantasy unbound by the patriarchal structures of the classic narrative or art cinema.

In *Johanna D'Arc* four women meet in the Trans-Siberian Railway dining car (and later change to the Trans-Mongolian): Lady Windermere (Delphine Seyrig), an elegant British anthropologist; Giovanna (Ines Sastre), a young adventure-seeker; Fanny Ziegfeld (Gillian Scalici), an American Broadway musical star; and Frau Muller-Vohwinkel (Irm Hermann), a hesitant German schoolmistress. Lady Windermere, lured by curiosity from her luxury accommodation to explore the third class compartments where soldiers, poor peasants, and Jewish refugees crowd together, encounters the young, beautiful Giovanna reclining in the overhead luggage rack, listening to her Sony walkman. In what must be one of the most subtle pick-ups in cinema history, Lady Windermere invites Giovanna back to share her first class compartment. The nature of the relationship is suggested visually, much in keeping with Ottinger's preference for images over sync-sound dialogue: we watch Lady Windermere watch Giovanna as she awakes the next morning, desire becoming palpable in Delphine Seyrig's expressive face. In a scene which occurs in the second, more documentary half of the film, Lady Windermere and Giovanna are riding a camel together across the expansive Mongolian landscape, Lady Windermere closely behind Giovanna, both positioned comfortably between the animal's two humps. It is this sort of suggestive imagery which plays on the lesbian imagination and takes the place of more didactic or conventional narrative strategies.

The erotic connection between the older, sophisticated woman and her ingenue adventurer is understated yet potent. It could, but never does, become diffused by the many richly layered textures, story-lines, and cultural references. As with *Madame X*, Ottinger is not concerned with character development or psychological motivation: she paints rich images which lead us not into the characters' psyches but outward, to a wide array of visual and emotional associations. The Kalinka Sisters, a Georgian musical trio, dress in outrageous matching costumes; the voluminous Yiddish performer Mickey Katz orders a vast amount of the most exotic Russian delicacies, the entertainment in the dining car is so well-choreographed and the *mise en scène* so perfectly developed that our senses become overwhelmed. Fanny Ziegfeld says admiringly of Mickey

Tabea Blumenschein plays the pirate queen and Ulrike Ottinger her tragic lover Orlando, in Ottinger's lesbian cult classic, *Madame X–An Absolute Ruler*.

Joanne D'Arc of Mongolia: The Kalinka Sisters provide evening entertainment in the Trans-Siberian Railway dining car.

Joanna D'Arc of Mongolia: Giovanna wakes up in Lady Windermere's first class sleeper-car the following morning.

Joanna D'Arc of Mongolia: A campy encounter between east and west in the Mongolian landscape.

Katz: 'You, my dear Katz, are in any case a large, conspicuous swatch of color in our monoculture.' This fascination with difference anticipates the encounter between Mongolian and western women soon to take place.

To say that the women on the Trans-Mongolian Railway are kidnapped by a tribe of Mongolian women and that their princess, Ulun Iga (Xu Re Huar), also takes a fancy to Giovanna, is to reduce a broadly engaging epic to only a few bones in the skeleton of its plot. But it does give a sense of the romantic power of the film, especially for women. Fiction-fantasy and ethnographic documentary perfectly unite, the fantasy demanding a pleasurable seduction and the slow, ethnographic pacing insisting on a cultural encounter for the spectator as well.

Patricia White points out that the promise of *Madame X*, of uncertainty and danger, but also love and adventure, 'sounds much like that of cinema itself – the guarantee of pleasure is the beautiful, cruel woman'.[39] Despite Ottinger's distance from and rejection of traditional (art or classic) cinema conventions, she still insists on visual pleasure dependent upon the image of woman – but this image of woman demands an intimate, erotic relationship with the female gaze. Rather than moralizing about the dominant constructions of sexuality or working toward 'the destruction of pleasure [for men] as a radical weapon' as Laura Mulvey has suggested, women's cinema would do better to imagine, as Ottinger has, new ways of constructing visual pleasure for women. Without this, women's cinema hardly seems necessary or desirable.

6

Transgressive Cinema: Lesbian Independent Film

A young, attractive woman exchanges looks with a nun on the streets of New York's Lower East Side. The nun walks away quickly, but the woman follows her right into a church. And the camera positions our view with that of the bold pursuer, so that we unexpectedly find ourselves guilty of transgressing the taboo, of looking at the nun somehow 'differently'. But at the same time, the camera's virtually frantic movement, while securing our gaze to that of someone walking quickly down an urban street, also frees our gaze from that which she sees (the nun), thereby disturbing the possibility of an erotic contemplation of the image. What occurs in this one short scene is that we are implicated in the romantic pursuit of a nun, yet the eroticism is not attributable to the object of the look, to the image of Woman to signify sexuality, as it would be in the dominant cinema or in pornography. It is rather the power and intrigue of looking itself which becomes erotically charged. Su Friedrich's *Damned If You Don't* (1987) has imagined lesbian desire outside of the pornographic parameters of the dominant cinema.

This goal – not often achieved – is a primary one for lesbian independent film, and one of its defining characteristics. The growing body of work referred to as lesbian independent cinema has been attempting to control and define lesbian representation in terms other than those offered by the dominant media. These films provide very different perspectives on lesbian desire and, with varying degrees of success, also subvert the ways in which the cinema historically has been constructed for the male gaze. Lesbian independent filmmaking attempts to construct alternative visual codes that more closely derive from the search for lesbian self-definition.

In the United States, lesbian independent film emerged in the early 1970s with the advent of the gay and women's liberation movements.

It benefited from a strengthening of the American independent film movement in general in the 1960s, a consequence of that decade's anti-establishment climate, the founding of such granting agencies as the National Endowment for the Arts (giving, however, only piecemeal funding for film production), and the technological development of lighter, more accessible 16mm film equipment. Although the production of lesbian films spans a number of western countries, the relative lack of government or television subsidy for independent work make for an independent film practice which is particularly American, unrecognized by and marginal to a massive, world-exporting Hollywood film industry. Only in the United States, for example, would the following grassroots fundraising announcement be found in a mid-1970s lesbian journal: 'Their budget is $25,000, and they need $5,000 to start the film.' This ad in *Lesbian Tide* was for what turned out to be perhaps the most widely screened and recognized lesbian documentary, Iris Films' *In the Best Interest of the Children*.[1] Some of the formal qualities developing out of this independent, marginal position have found their way into the films of non-American western directors, just as the codes of European art cinema have become discernible in American films. However, lesbian independent films are situated differently in Canada and Europe due to the existence (now unfortunately changing) of complete government or television production subsidy and, in continental western Europe, a history that fostered a national film culture. In Britain, lesbian films have not had to resort to this kind of panhandling within the lesbian community and have been commissioned for television broadcast virtually without exception, a situation that carries with it certain aesthetic and audience mandates – one thinks of Beeban Kidron's *Oranges Are Not the Only Fruit* (U.K., 1989), Joy Chamberlain's *Nocturne* (U.K., 1990), Pratibha Parmar's *Flesh and Paper* (U.K., 1990). Although there is much that could be said about these works, my focus here is on American films which in form and content declare their complete independence from and opposition to the dominant American film and television industries.

Inspired by the energy and enthusiasm of the 1970s lesbian/feminist movement, the first significant lesbian independent films proclaimed their allegiance to this movement by visually articulating its utopian agenda. Pioneering lesbian filmmakers Barbara Hammer and Jan Oxenberg began in the early 1970s to make short personal films that affirmed their experiences and sexuality, Oxenberg drawing upon narrative and documentary styles and Hammer upon the avant garde film tradition. *Dyketactics* by

Barbara Hammer (1974) and *Home Movie* by Jan Oxenberg (1972) both share the early movement's insistence that lesbianism is not solely a personal, sexual matter, but is a form of social or political liberation. These and other lesbian films from this period had in common their conscious attempts to address a specifically lesbian audience, by relying on the audience's familiarity with the cultural assumptions, symbolism, humor, and radical politics characteristic of the American lesbian-feminist community at that time.

For some filmmakers who subscribed to the lesbian separatist tendencies of the movement and wanted to protect these new images from male appropriation, the film's mode of address was not enough; they insisted on further exclusion of the male viewer by showing their films in women-only spaces, the women's centers and coffeehouses that sprang up across the United States during the early 1970s. Journals such as *Lesbian Tide* and *Amazon Quarterly* carried regular announcements of Barbara Hammer's films, invariably ending with 'this program is for wimmin, only'.[2] Jan Oxenberg, interviewed in *Amazon Quarterly*, said of one of her films, 'Now, this film is not . . . for the general public. It's really entertainment for the lesbian community. As far as I'm concerned, it's not being made for other people to see.'[3]

Jan Oxenberg and Barbara Hammer are filmmakers who represented two (frequently overlapping) tendencies within 1970s lesbian-feminism, which could be differentiated by the terms 'cultural feminism' and 'radical feminism'. Both tendencies imbued the definition of lesbianism with significance beyond the sexual: beginning with the Radicalesbians in 1970, 'lesbian' began to suggest 'woman-identified' in both a personal and political sense.[4] But whereas radical feminists emphasized the political importance of 'woman-identified-women' as a threat to patriarchy and as an antidote to male power, cultural feminists moved away from immediate political concerns to explore ancient matriarchies and female forms of power. Radical feminists argued that, given the narrow patriarchal definitions of woman, being 'feminine' and being a whole person are irreconcilable,[5] while cultural feminists embraced the feminine in themselves, and connected lesbianism to the creative, eternal feminine principle. Cultural feminists tried to create a women's culture that came as close to lesbian nirvana and kept as far from patriarchal realities as possible, which radical feminists sometimes criticized as a retreat.[6]

Home Movie takes up the radical feminist position that lesbianism is an antidote to male power. Rather than situate her film completely within a female community (as Barbara Hammer's early films are situated), Oxenberg juxtaposes, and in the course of the short film replaces, images of patriarchal order with images of lesbian pleasure. The film uses home movies of the filmmaker's childhood to call into question the heterosexual socialization process of childhood; familiar images of a little girl dancing for the camera and holding a doll are given new meaning via the soundtrack, in which the filmmaker asks, 'I wonder why I was doing this? I look so ... normal, just like a little girl. And it's really strange, because I didn't feel like a little girl.' Over the home movies of herself as a teenager, cheerleading at a high school football game, the filmmaker's voice continues to undermine the conventional reading of the image: 'The thing I liked best about being a cheerleader was being with the other cheerleaders.' As Michelle Citron points out,

> Oxenberg uses home movies to underscore the role of the family and school as institutions that perpetuate patriarchal ideology. In the context of this film, home movies, usually a celebratory recording of family life, ironically become a condemnation of the very institutions filmed.[7]

Not only, as Citron argues, does *Home Movie* directly critique patriarchal ideology, placing it within the radical feminist camp, but it also sees a problematic, even contradictory relationship between the identities 'lesbian' and 'feminine'. Oxenberg's lesbianism, as indicated by her commentary about not feeling like a little girl, is signaled by her difference from a culturally-mandated feminine model, not by identification with a natural, eternal feminine principle. If 'feminine' and 'whole person' are irreconcilable, the choice is clear. By the end of the film, the woman has abandoned her efforts to fit in to a socially sanctioned role, and this abandonment is depicted in 'liberating' imagery. No longer cheering on the sidelines, she is playing a sensuous, non-competitive, disorderly game of football with a group of lesbians, an image of strength and a celebration of women's 'non-feminine' bodies.

In contrast, Barbara Hammer's work can be seen as embodying the cultural feminist position.[8] Her many lesbian-identified films of this period involve the quest for a lesbian iconography, a visual language not defined by the heterosexual, patriarchal world, but rather based on personal inner truths and the rhythms of her own body. She worked from an intuitive, 'female' source of knowledge, claiming that 'my body tells me how to shoot or how to edit. I work with a kinesthetic feeling rather than an a-priori plan

Barbara Hammer begins her search for a lesbian visual language with *Dyketactics* (1974).

The primacy of touch in *Dyketactics*.

when it comes to the way I want to express myself with the camera.'[9] The lesbian self and lesbian sexuality, long erased from the visual history of patriarchy, became visible in Barbara Hammer's work through matriarchal images and symbols of women's spirituality, a connection with 'female' nature (as opposed to 'male' culture), and a focus on the lesbian body as a source of power and knowledge, themes which had considerable currency in early and mid-1970s American lesbian communities. In a prolific body of work with such titles as *Moon Goddess, Sappho, Sisters!, Women I Love, Menses, Women's Rites, Multiple Orgasm* and *The Great Goddess*, Hammer favored the use of superimposition and a linkage of vaginal and nature imagery, connecting women's bodies to ancient spiritual sites or natural formations, and always, to each other.

Jacqueline Zita describes Hammer's agenda as follows:

> To invert the cultural negations and denials attached to the lesbian body seems the first task at hand. There are two obvious possibilities: the body that has been historically defiled and abhorred can become purified, sanctified, and turned into an object of worship, or the body that has become denigrated as unnatural and sick can be 'naturalized' and normalized to fit more intimately into the rhythms of Nature ... Both of these tendencies are present in Barbara's films.[10]

While Barbara Hammer evolved her own particular, lyrical style within the predominantly male avant garde, other lesbian filmmakers drew upon more conventional film forms. The 1970s and early 80s saw the creation of an unprecedented range of low-budget independent films which utilized many film styles. Short personal narratives predominated, focusing on first 'coming out', initiating relationships, or depicting everyday personal experiences.[11] Although 'positive' in their presentations of lesbianism, these films did not always subscribe to the cultural feminists' utopian lesbian ideal, and often highlighted conflicts that lesbians experienced, if not with each other then at least with the heterosexual world. For example, Greta Schiller's first film, *Greta's Girls* (1977), creates a fictional day in the life of a young interracial (white and black) lesbian couple, whose everyday trials of urban life (hassles at the bank, an uncooperative dog, lewd male comments at the hardware store, blown electric fuses) are presented as part of how lesbians 'really live' and are offset by the affection of the two women for each other.

Documentaries from the 1970s, often collectively produced, also celebrated lesbian lifestyles and usually grounded lesbian experience more directly in political realities. Iris Films' *In the Best Interest of the Children*

(1978) confronts and challenges the devastating homophobia that separates lesbian mothers from their children, while presenting a realistic picture of individual lesbian lives. The film interviews women who are articulate, interesting and extremely vulnerable (their custody of their children can always be contested by husbands, parents, or the state); they are at once ordinary and remarkable women, with a heroism you can't help but admire. In this sense the film offers a 'positive image' of lesbians, but it is not a flat, propagandist one; a range of individuals and conflicts are explored to create a rich tapestry of lesbian experience.

The documentaries, however, usually found themselves in a difficult position that other lesbian films of the period could more easily avoid: of trying to appeal to a lesbian audience while carrying the added burden of a mission for social change, a goal which entailed reaching and influencing the heterosexual world. *In the Best Interest of the Children* takes up pro-lesbian values, and presents 'real-life' lesbians with whom lesbian viewers could identify. But the film also assumed an organizing and educational function to change attitudes surrounding lesbian motherhood, and in fact the film was widely used by social service agencies and in lesbian custody battles. As a result of this need to speak two languages at once, as it were, the film at times promotes and at other times compromises its radical feminist politics, for example giving the impression that lesbian moms feed their children Wonder Bread just like straight moms do, hardly a position to be appreciated by most lesbian-feminists of the mid-1970s, who didn't care to emulate the heterosexual nuclear family model.

If early lesbian documentaries were intended as correctives to the dominant culture's myths about lesbians, lesbian avant garde films were often intended as correctives to dominant representations of lesbian sexuality. These films experimented with non-voyeuristic approaches to lesbian sexuality: for example, in Barbara Hammer's *Dyketactics* and *Women I Love*, the filmmaker is participant instead of voyeur of lesbian lovemaking, while in Su Friedrich's *Gently Down the Stream*, words scratched into the film's emulsion take precedence over images occupying only a corner of the frame. Whereas Chantal Akerman's lesbian lovemaking scene in *Je Tu Il Elle* stars the filmmaker in order to de-aestheticize the lesbian image, Hammer's use of her own body is integral to the lesbian sensibility she was then developing. Akerman's much cooler (anti-)aesthetic in her lovemaking scene is precariously balanced between her strict control as director and her vulnerability as performer, while Hammer's performance in her own films from this period lacks that feeling of vulnerability – and her directing lacks that strict control. There isn't the same tension in

Hammer's dual role of filmmaker and performer; they are part of one tactile relationship to the image. As Jacqueline Zita has noted, the filmmaker's participation

> gives the camera itself an altogether different role. Instead of being used to gaze upon the spectacle, it seems to be part of the action, used to capture a loving intimacy by connecting with it and completing its fleeting and primitive pleasure ... Barbara's camera is subjective; it participates as does the filmmaker in an orchestrated event between two bodies and a camera.[12]

The filmmaker's participation in the lovemaking scene is not enough alone to counteract the prevalent construction of lesbian lovemaking as cinematic spectacle designed to titillate male desire. But it does begin to break down the barriers between spectators, filmmaker, and image upon which voyeurism relies. Hammer's inclusion of her own body serves a further purpose, to rely on the personal truths of her own body (the only 'reliable' source under patriarchy) in order to give universal expression to the lesbian body.

By the early 1980s, feminism had evolved, and so had lesbian independent cinema, which was now starting to embrace more complex theoretical and aesthetic questions. Some feminists had started to question a feminist politic that reinscribed femininity as an essence, as biological and natural rather than historically and culturally constructed, a position which ultimately returns to the place patriarchal culture has assigned to women: outside of culture, in the realm of the emotions, nature, and motherhood. Working class lesbians and lesbians of color found themselves excluded from both the luxury of utopian, separatist lifestyles and from a 'universal' lesbian mythology extrapolated from specific, personal (primarily white middle class) lesbian identity, while more androgynous or 'masculine' women were unable to fit within the rigid parameters required by the cult of the feminine. As these voices grew stronger, utopian fantasies eventually gave way to diversity and conflict.

Meanwhile, issues of sexuality and sexual representation were heating up in the early 1980s, dividing the feminist movement into hostile camps on opposite sides of the pornography debate. In the 1970s, feminists viewed pornography rather simply as visual propaganda which advocated violence against women, but then neither pornography nor violence against women received much critical attention outside of feminist circles. By the early 1980s, they, as Dot Tuer so bluntly put it, found their struggles co-opted by a moral majority who stepped over battered bodies of women in their rush to manipulate public opinion.[13]

As the New Right moved in on what had been feminist territory, many women were unhappy about feminism's strange new bedfellows, and had serious doubts about whether censorship or 'pro-family' values were any improvement over pornography. The issue was realigning itself as pro or anti-sex, and many lesbians, rebelling against the political correctness and puritanical aspects of the lesbian-feminist movement, suddenly came out as pro-sex in all its variations of pleasure and perversion. The direct visual representation of these ideas about sexuality is limited primarily to photography and to low-low-budget home video pornography for lesbians (such as those by Blush Productions). The government funding bodies had long overlooked lesbian artists and their proposed film projects; by the late 1980s they were demanding anti-obscenity pledges from all artists receiving government monies. But while this new preoccupation with sex has not become the primary concern for lesbian filmmakers, the visual representations created by the lesbian porn movement and these other changes taking place within the lesbian community still have considerable ramifications for lesbian independent film.

One significant development in recent documentary film is that the idea of a 'universal', transhistorical lesbian has been replaced with lesbian specificity and diversity. The lives of lesbians who would have been overlooked or ridiculed by 1970s lesbian-feminists for role-playing, 'male-identification' or just not conforming to the feminine ideal, are now documented and celebrated. Storme deLarverie, the subject of Michelle Parkerson's documentary, *Storme: The Lady of the Jewel Box* (1987) is one such woman: she is the talented male impersonator who from 1955 to 1969 fronted the once-famous, multi-racial drag show, the *Jewel Box Revue*.

Storme lets the woman speak for herself, and what she says reveals her inner strength and her refusal to change for other people's approval: 'I grew up hard in New Orleans with my mixed blood. So I was my own responsibility ... All I had to do was just be me, and let people use their imaginations. It never changed me.' Her powerful words give a very different history from the media headlines Parkerson has uncovered of Storme's heyday, which were preoccupied with 'Lads in Drag and One Mustachioed Girl, Or Limp-Wrist Time on Broadway'.

But the very process of reclaiming the history behind the headlines is invariably thwarted by its attempt to represent that which the dominant culture would rather erase. As a documentary rather than fiction filmmaker, Parkerson does not have the freedom of Monique Wittig's approach to history:

> ... You say there are no words to describe this time, you say it does not exist. But remember. Make an effort to remember. Or, failing that, invent.[14]

Parkerson confronted the film archives, the official visual memory bank of history, and found no moving images to describe the transgressive phenomenon of the *Jewel Box Revue*, no evidence that it ever existed. She never successfully circumvented this huge obstacle, and indeed, how could she? Although the story of Storme is fascinating, the film is visually handicapped, an outstanding example of how lesbians, and particularly non-white, working-class lesbians, threatening on so many levels to the social order, are virtually unrepresentable within the dominant culture. Perhaps influenced by this experience, Parkerson's new film *Litany* (produced by Ada Griffin and currently in post-production), does not have to depend upon the official historical record; as a portrait of the black lesbian poet, Audre Lorde, it had easy access to Audre's poetry, friends, daily life, and footage of contemporary movements in which she played an important part.

The absence of archival images with which to visualize the lesbian past is a problem that manifested itself over and over in the huge research project undertaken for Greta Schiller's feature length documentary, *Before Stonewall* (1984), on which I worked as research director. The brief of the film was lesbian and gay history, and we worked to make sure lesbians would be visible and not overshadowed by the far more available history of gay men. We were committed to locating a range of lesbian representation, including racial diversity, working class experience, closeted and 'out', 'butch' and 'femme', victim and survivor. In part this meant looking at images differently, and seeing what was left out. I wrote at the time, 'the process of unearthing a gay iconography involves seeing with double vision. Absence as image. Erasure as image.'[15]

In one of my subsequent collaborations with Greta Schiller, *Tiny & Ruby: Hell Divin' Women* (1988), a portrait of two jazz musicians who had been living and playing music together for over 40 years, we encountered similar problems of erasure from history. Despite Tiny Davis's fame within the black community in the 1940s, when she received media-billing as the 'female Louis Armstrong', film footage of her simply did not exist.

We tried to find visual and narrative solutions to the problem of

Greta Schiller on location with the "girls" in her first film, *Greta's Girls* (1977).

Attempting to document black lesbian history: *Tiny & Ruby: Hell Divin' Women* by Greta Schiller and Andrea Weiss.

black lesbian documentation. Like Michelle Parkerson, we used video-animation to try to bring photographs to life. We placed an image of Tiny and Ruby over archival footage in which they did not appear, pointing out their erasure from the historical record and the impossibility of inserting them back in. And we collaborated with black lesbian poet Cheryl Clarke, whose narrative poetry created a context for viewing their lives in a rich oral tradition of black women's stories. One critic wrote of the film that 'the poetry, like the filmmaking, seems to continue the work – although in a different form – of women like Tiny Davis and Ruby Lucas.'[16] But how well these strategies work is a personal question; for most viewers the vivaciousness and outrageousness of Tiny and Ruby themselves come across regardless, giving first-person immediacy to the broader issues of race, lesbian experience, role-playing, and creativity, and the relation of these issues to historical invisibility. Ultimately Tiny's and Ruby's lives, like Storme's, do not depend upon the 'correction' of the historical record; they, and the films celebrating them, are precisely concerned with a very different idea of history and experience. As Helen Fehervary has noted, 'The relationship between history and so-called subjective processes is not a matter of grasping the truth in history as some objective entity, but in finding the truth of the experience. Evidently, this kind of experiential immediacy has to do with women's own history and self-consciousness.'[17]

Attending the 1989 Berlin Film Festival screening of *Tiny & Ruby* on a double bill with Isaac Julien's *Looking for Langston* (U.K., 1988), a short, black and white lyrical meditation on gay life in the Harlem Renaissance, caused me to reflect on the contrast between a developing black gay male aesthetic in the cinema and the absence of a black lesbian equivalent.[18] The visual contrast between the cool, elegantly stylized black gay male image in *Looking for Langston* and the more intimate, less polished lesbian image in either *Tiny & Ruby* or *Storme* is more than can simply be explained by the financial realities of the American independent sector, especially for lesbian projects – realities that Isaac Julien's far better funded British film did not have to confront. The totally opposite aesthetic approach taken by the two films in that Berlin program forcibly suggests that gay male filmmakers have a very different relation to erotic representation as well as a different historical legacy; they are not bound in their exploration of a visual aesthetic by such lesbian concerns as the overwhelming appropriation of the female body for advertising and male erotic pleasure, concerns which might make such glamorized images highly suspect for lesbian filmmakers.

The representation of black lesbians in independent narrative films is obviously not subjected to the same constraints as in historical documentary. Lizzie Borden's *Born in Flames* (1983) combines 1970s radical feminist politics with a focus on diversity among and differences between women, especially along racial lines, which penetrated feminist thought more consistently in the 1980s. Although the film brings together black, white, Latina, and Asian women characters of different ages, it is especially striking for the power and beauty with which it represents black women, especially through the characters of Adelaide Norris (Jean Satterfield), Zella Wylie (Flo Kennedy) and Honey (Honey), who represent the vanguard of feminism in terms of both political theory and action.

The power of black women in this film is not the power that white American culture has long attributed to relatively powerless black women, the 'matriarchal' status that white culture has assigned to black women's lives simply because of their insubordination to black men.[19] The film discredits this cultural mythology in one of its first scenes, where with intended irony we are given the 'matriarchal' family background of a black feminist revolutionary as seen by the dominant culture: poverty, female-headed household, eight kids, are all here. Nor is the beauty with which black women are represented that of traditional aestheticized female images, extended since the 1960s to black women but still based on narrow definitions of femininity and race. The power and beauty that black women in *Born in Flames* emanate, through their insistence on taking power into their own hands, and their physical strength and comfort in their bodies, stands in sharp contradiction to and serves to dismantle these cultural constructions of race and gender.

Born in Flames is a low-budget feature set in what looks like the present, but, we learn, is ten years after a peaceful socialist democratic revolution has taken place in the United States, leaving the basic structures of patriarchy intact. Refusing to be appeased any longer, a 'women's army' becomes increasingly militant in its actions against the government, eventually taking over the news media. The narrative is disjunctive, cutting back and forth between several groups of women (representing different feminist tendencies which will eventually unite), between a diverse range of 'languages', musical and spoken (punk rock, blues, rap music, informal 'black' English, media newspeak, political theory) and between various levels of visual representation which offer different perspectives on the same event.

First we see what seems to be an 'insider's' view of the interaction between the women, and then the scene cuts to an image in which this interaction is monitored by the government (police or FBI), to its being debated by other groups of women, and finally to its distortion beyond recognition by the media. In one particularly striking shot, a black and white erotically charged image whose graininess conceals as well as reveals, two naked women's bodies slowly move in concert with each other. But our enjoyment of the image is disrupted as we encounter a freeze-frame and a male voice (which we recognize as that of an FBI agent) is heard; the image becomes a slide projected in FBI headquarters. This shift in representation makes a strong point about how women's personal lives are extremely vulnerable to political surveillance and state regulation, and further suggests our lack of control over the appropriation of lesbian images.

The changes in feminist thinking about sexuality across the decade of the 1980s can be discerned in Lizzie Borden's career. *Born in Flames* is, among other things, a cautionary tale about the appropriation of women's bodies, while Borden's next film, *Working Girls* (1986) – about women who work in the sex industry but are 'in control' instead of victims – can be found in the porn section of your local video store. What began as a feminist approach to sexual representation was readily appropriated in its marketing campaign as white-collar pornography, in which feminists and 'sophisticated' men can find common ground.

Sheila McLaughlin's *She Must Be Seeing Things* (1987) is the American independent film which most directly draws upon lesbian fascination with sexual taboos in the 1980s. The film takes a fairly conventional narrative form, with continuity editing, suspenseful music, fantasy sequences and a film-within-a-film. These characteristics place it more closely within the realist European art cinema than within the American independent 'new-narrative' film, which usually takes a less linear approach to story-telling and a more fractured approach to characterization. The narrative of *She Must Be Seeing Things* centers on a relationship between two women, a black lawyer, Agatha (Sheila Dabney) and a white independent filmmaker, Jo (Lois Weaver). Agatha reads Jo's diary, which is a litany of her compulsive sexual escapades with men, and this sets off Agatha's jealousy and distrust of Jo. Her fantasy is that she will murder Jo in revenge for her sexual infidelities. The fantasy sequences and Agatha's spying on Jo provide the opportunity to offer virtually something for everyone: voyeurism, bondage, heterosexual sex, butch-femme role-playing, fetishism, crossdressing, exhibitionism.

This variety-pack approach to sexuality has the unintended conse-quence of reducing it all to a mere matter of 'sexual preference', of equally available private lifestyle choices – an approach that tends to diminish the radical implications of the very concepts of sexual difference and its representation that the film takes as its agenda. And yet the film's presentation of sexuality is not even one of liberal 'equal opportunity'; the double standard of heterosexuality prevails. In terms of lesbian sensuality, we see Agatha and Jo together in a seduction scene that is cut short by a broken record on the stereo; affectionate on the beach; and physically playful in a beautifully filmed but unsatisfying closing shot of the two of them on a city street. This ending seems to resolve too neatly all that has gone on before and to reduce lesbian desire to good, clean girlish fun. On the other hand, all of the explicit and implied sexual scenes are invariably heterosexual, whether within Agatha's fantasies, Jo's journal, or the film-within-a-film which Jo is directing. Sheila McLaughlin has said of her film: 'I was trying to deal openly with the ultimate lesbian horror, the fantasy of having sex with a man.'[20] While the representation of a range of sexual expressions for women can be applauded, has lesbian sexuality become so commonplace, its representation so mainstream, that it is redundant to include it in a film that claims to be about lesbian desire? Or are lesbians so sheltered from the omnipresent images of heterosexual sex that unrelenting scenarios of heterosexual sex are now shocking? Threatening?

The film's reliance on strict characterization can further work against its pleasure for lesbian spectators. It is revealing to compare *She Must Be Seeing Things* with Lizzie Borden's *Born in Flames*, which uses diverse cultural and subcultural discourses and spectator positions. These strategies allow viewers to engage with the film through many different kinds of identification. As Teresa de Lauretis has observed,

> That the audience is conceived as a heterogeneous community is made apparent, in Borden's film, by its unusual handling of the function of address. The use of music and beat in conjunction with spoken language, from rap singing to a variety of subcultural lingos and nonstandard speech, serves ... what in another context might be called characterization: they are there to provide a means of identification of and with the characters, though not the kind of psychological identification usually accorded to main characters or privileged 'protagonists'.[21]

In contrast, *She Must Be Seeing Things* relies on traditional processes of character identification. Since the character of Jo is visually coded as 'heterosexual', and for many lesbian viewers she may well be an unsympathetic character (alcoholic, manipulative, no female friends,

Lizzie Borden's *Born in Flames:* Especially striking for the power and beauty with which it represents black lesbians.

Jo and Angela in Sheila McLaughlin's *She Must Be Seeing Things*. In this rare moment of closeness, their eyes still don't meet.

flirtatious with men), the film effectively blocks one of the only two means of entry into it, namely, via the two protagonists.

At first, the film seems refreshing for its attempt to represent an interracial relationship and 'butch-femme' dynamics, both of which are lesbian experiences rarely discussed and virtually never visually depicted. On both of these terrains, McLaughlin is charting new filmic territory. But unfortunately, neither attempt fully succeeds. 'Butch-femme' has a rich erotic heritage among lesbians, and *She Must Be Seeing Things* displaces the identity of the 'femme' onto a heterosexual woman, giving it a completely different meaning and erasing altogether the already less visible part of the equation.[22] In terms of the interracial dynamics, the film barely acknowledges them. As Martha Gever points out,

> . . . the racial and cultural differences that the two women embody remain understated in the film . . . Instead, Agatha and Jo are assumed to inhabit a shared culture, which constitutes a utopia in light of the fact of racial inequity in U.S. society.[23]

Finally, unlike *Born in Flames*, *She Must Be Seeing Things* relies on the dominant culture's aestheticized images of women, black or white. Jo is the traditional WASP 'blonde bombshell', with platinum hair, tight skirt, and heels, while Agatha is the glamorized black female image that finds itself in the pages of *Essence* magazine: straight hair, well-groomed and dressed for a success most black women will never be allowed to achieve. While the film rejects the narcissistic sameness between women that predominated in earlier, more utopian lesbian films of the 1970s, it aligns their differences with two mainstream cultural definitions of femininity. It is important to acknowledge, as Sheila McLaughlin does in an interview about her film, that

> Heterosexuality is the dominant code of the society that we live in, and it defines and in a sense creates our own sexuality, whether we choose to participate as literally heterosexual or not.[24]

But this reality does not doom us to endless variations on heterosexual images, heterosexual scenarios, and heterosexual rules governing the female body; the dominant culture is not so absolute or unassailable as all that. Whereas the power and beauty of women's bodies in *Born in Flames* come from a source far different from that of the dominant culture's mandates, *She Must Be Seeing Things*, while seemingly arguing just the opposite, ends up affirming the position that lesbians too can find fulfillment in heterosexual sex and heterosexual definitions of womanhood.

In assessing contemporary lesbian independent film, it seems that experimental film forms lend themselves more readily than documentary or narrative to exploring possibilities for and problems in the visual expression of lesbian desire. Although this is not meant to disparage documentary and narrative filmmaking, it does seem that experimental, or avant garde, film is able to circumvent both the historical problems of documentary film and the repression of lesbianism by classic narrative film conventions, which has insidiously found its way into independent narratives as well.

This is a position which Barbara Hammer alludes to when she asks whether 'radical content requires radical form', a question that presupposes that the avant garde is indeed radical, and not also burdened by a heavily masculinist, heterosexist bias, and that documentary and narrative forms are necessarily conventional.[25] This debate cannot be taken up in full here, but Hammer's question is part of her ongoing refinement of a lesbian aesthetic developed within her large body of work. *Sync Touch* (1981) can be seen as Hammer's treatise on lesbian filmmaking, in which she attempts to define in more theoretical terms the aesthetic concerns pervading her work since *Dyketactics* in 1974.

Sync Touch is structured in four sections, each exploring the relationship between touch and sight which the film maintains is the basis for lesbian filmmaking. The first section utilizes handpainted and pixolated photographic images, a rapid montage of finger-painted 16mm frames and contact sheets. The textures of the paint break up and dominate the image, but we see recognizable images fleetingly emerging and disappearing: one is of Hammer hugging her camera, another is of a blindfolded woman and girl sitting at a film projector. Both images convey the primacy of touch over sight, the first for the (female) filmmaking process, the second for the (female) spectator as well.

This idea is developed further in the third section of the film, in which what we conventionally call the 'image' is from an old erotic film of Hammer. Here the erotic potential is obscured by the physical, tactile properties of the film medium itself, which prove the stronger: the jumpiness and graininess of the image, the scratches, sprocket holes, emulsion and visible frameline dominate the screen and comprise the 'true' image. At one point the film slips in the optical printer gate and becomes completely abstract.

In the film's final sequence, two women are face to face, one (the filmmaker) repeating after the other a French statement about feminism and language. The English subtitles read:

Feminist language is complete. It reunites mind and body, intellect and reason to physical sensation and emotion . . . We are in a culture where expression of the heart and the senses are repressed. The heart of the film is the rapport between touch and sight.

This French lesson which concludes the film connects Hammer's articulation of her lesbian aesthetic to French feminism, especially suggesting Luce Irigaray's 'When Our Lips Speak Together' (1977), which also insists on the primacy of touch, not sight, in the construction of female sexuality, and which also connotes strong lesbian associations.

Sync Touch was the last film Barbara Hammer made before turning away from explicitly lesbian imagery to explore other visual concerns throughout the 1980s. As Claudia Gorbman has written of her work following *Sync Touch*, 'Her recent films . . . have virtually absented human forms; instead they focus on women's vision, a woman's vision, translating/interpreting/transforming the world.'[26] In *Sync Touch* Hammer's long association of visual and tactile senses continues but her previous focus on the lesbian body has changed. In the second section (a lecture on touch, filmed using a macro lens to create an extreme close-up of the speaker) she eroticizes the face; in the third section she obscures the body; in the fourth section she clothes the body and conveys an eroticism through ideas. This last section (the French lesson) visually pairs the two women. They are clothed similarly, both have short brown hair, wear long earrings, and are facing each other; then are facing the camera in a close-up on their eyebrows and eyes, again visually paired. This section continues a lesbian sensibility that was by 1981 rapidly changing – differences between women began to carry a far stronger erotic charge. But other changes occurring in lesbian representation are here: it is clear in the film that the representation of the lesbian body has become far more problematic than its celebration in her films from the 1970s ever implied; perhaps Hammer also felt the need to protect it from the fetishization and voyeurism now also the province of lesbians. In any case, the film takes a strong step toward 'displacing' the lesbian body with other kinds of imagery, foreshadowing the change to come, a change which Gorbman describes: 'the lesbian body has moved out of the frame to the camera's viewfinder.'[27]

Su Friedrich's *Gently Down the Stream*, made the same year as *Sync Touch*, also involves a highly tactile approach to the filmmaking process and also deals with erotic content in a way which obscures rather than reveals women's bodies. The film is black and white and silent, and into

With *Sync Touch* (1981), Barbara Hammer reassessed the meaning of the lesbian body in patriarchal culture.

black leader Friedrich has scratched words that, one at a time, construct a narrative which recounts the filmmaker's dreams. Although the words serve this narrative function, they work more prominently as a visual image themselves, and one which, as they scratch and disturb the film's emulsion, has strong tactile qualities. As with Hammer's optical printing of an erotic film in *Sync Touch*, the erotic potential of Friedrich's dreams is subjugated to the film's physical properties. The photographic images which intermittently appear have a dream-like association rather than literal relationship to these words.

In one of the dream narratives, we see in the upper right corner an image of a woman on a rowing machine, while we read that: 'A woman sits on a stage hunched over in the corner. She calls up a friend from the audience, asking her: [and at this point the image in the corner disappears, the words occupy full screen, one word at a time] come and make love to me. She does. I can't watch. [The screen goes black for a moment, then in big, full-screen scratched letters] Moans MOANS ROARS roars HOWLS.' This sequence effectively raises a double edged concern: that of the filmic representation of women's sexuality, which it problematizes by banishing the image of the woman from the screen, and that of women's position as film spectator (a position that invariably implicates women in the voyeuristic process), which is problematized by the words 'I can't watch', followed by a blackened screen. These concerns are ones Friedrich takes up again and develops more fully in *Damned If You Don't* (1984).

Damned If You Don't successfully avoids the two major traps in which lesbian independent cinema has so often been caught over the past two decades: the 'essentialist' trap, on the one hand, that imagines lesbianism to be completely outside of patriarchal definitions and, on the other hand, the trap that situates lesbianism so strictly within patriarchal definitions that it can't imagine any way out from them. In re-imagining lesbian desire, *Damned If You Don't* interrogates the sexual definitions and mandates of the dominant culture and its institutions (specifically the cinema and the Catholic Church) and ultimately dismantles them so that a different story can be told.

Four distinct narratives are interwoven, some spoken and some told visually, three referring to events in the (historical or fictional) past, and one taking place in the film's present. In the film's present, the narrative focuses on the nun (Peggy Healey) and her attractive neighbor (Ela Troyano) whom we met at the beginning of this chapter. This narrative, told visually in a black and white style that is at once impressionistic and

Gently Down the Stream

documentary, moves from an exchange of looks, through a romantic pursuit, to the nun's discovery and reluctant acceptance of 'hitherto unsuspected emotions', to the seduction and lovemaking scene which ends the film.

The other three narratives consist of a condensed, rephotographed version of the 1946 Powell-Pressburger film, *Black Narcissus*, watched on a poor quality black and white television set by the neighbor/seductress (with an added female voice narrating the plot for us); a woman's off-screen, spoken recollections of nuns in Catholic high school and their importance to the awakening of her sexuality; and the reading aloud from the testimony of Sister Mea Crivelli regarding her 'immodest acts' with Sister Benedetta during the Renaissance. The situating of these three narratives in the near or far, historical or fictional past – 17th century, high school memories, a movie from the Forties with a foregone, unchangeable conclusion – enables us to view the film's present narrative as a sort of contemporary remake of these (hi)stories, with the possibility of a more satisfying resolution, in which desire can be rewarded instead of punished.

The original, color Powell-Pressburger film, *Black Narcissus* – although itself not exactly 'mainstream' in its use of cinema conventions – upholds the mainstream cinema's strict codification of Woman as good/bad, moral/immoral. But the way it is used here, as the film-within-the-film, in its condensed black and white silent version on a television with a female voice-over narration, challenges the dominant cinema's construction of sexual difference and its reliance on cultural binarism. Breaking the narrative into fragments on a TV screen and providing a voice-over narration completely alters our relation to the events of the film. First, the poor quality of the image disturbs rather than creates visual pleasure, and directs the viewer more strongly toward the spoken narration – narration which clearly spells out, and thereby deconstructs, the good nun/bad nun polarization, a process which is further assisted by the film's conversion from its original color to the more oppositional black and white. The dark gray horizontal bands which pass over the TV screen, at times forming a kind of black-out bar over the 'bad' nun's eyes to signify illicit behavior, serve this same purpose of exposing the ideological apparatus.

Second, by playing the film as a TV movie being watched by the nun's neighbor, *Damned If You Don't* inscribes the position of the lesbian spectator within the character of this unnamed woman. Her interest wanes during the course of *Black Narcissus*, perhaps due to the inevitability of the plot (the 'bad' nun is punished for her sexual desire, and in a struggle with the 'good' nun, falls over a cliff). By the film-within-a-film's end, the

Su Friedrich's *Damned If You Don't*: Identifying with the wrong character in *Black Narcissus*.

Violating the taboo: A woman seduces a nun in Su Friedrich's *Damned If You Don't*.

'bad' nun is dead and the unnamed woman is asleep, her identification with the 'wrong' character, the 'bad' nun, firmly established in a shot of her sleeping, surrounded by burning candles, which could possibly also be read as a shot of the 'bad' nun laid out for her funeral.

The two verbally revealed narratives in *Damned If You Don't* challenge the ideological construction and regulation of women's sexuality on another front besides the cinema – here, *Damned If You Don't* takes on the Catholic Church. In conversation with the filmmaker, a woman recalls her fascination with the eroticism with which Catholicism is imbued; her comments underscore Michel Foucault's position that sexual repression, far from subduing desire, fuels its obsession. In the readings from *Immodest Acts: The Life of a Lesbian Nun in Renaissance Italy*, the testimony of Sister Mea Crivelli, used to indict and imprison Sister Benedetta for the rest of her life (some thirty years), veils explicitly sexual content in moral language ('she corrupted herself, she corrupted me . . . '), which has the effect of doubling as confessional pornography. The linkage of the testimony against the lesbian nun with confessional pornography exposes the hypocrisy of the moral/immoral binary which could cast Sister Crivelli as the 'good' nun and Sister Benedetta as the 'bad' nun of this history. The reading of this testimony, interspersed with silence, over images of the nun (of the film's present) riding the subway and visiting Coney Island further breaks down this polarization which is central to the regulation of sexuality. The nun's initial exploration of desire involves looking through symbolic barriers: out of the train window, through sunglasses, through glass aquarium walls, and finally through the vertical convent bars behind which she is imprisoned – she watches the woman who first watched her.

The slow building to the seduction scene, the silence of the women's interaction, and the tension of the taboo being violated all contribute to the eroticism of the final scene in *Damned If You Don't*. The complicated removal of the nun's habit, in itself a liberating metaphor, sustains the eroticism by postponing its enactment. The women start to make love, and shortly after that the film ends, the suggestion all the more powerful for its not being culminated on the screen.

Afterword

T*he women start to make love, and shortly after that the film ends, the suggestion all the more powerful for its not being culminated on the screen.*

The previous sentence points to some major problems and contradictions in any attempt to construct a history of lesbian representation. After all, if a goal of current lesbian independent cinema is to represent the unrepresentable, to counter the dominant cinema's erasure and repression of lesbianism with open and available images, why would the suggestion of two women making love be all the more powerful for *not* being visually realized on the screen? With the relative availability of lesbian images in the 1980s and into the 90s, in art cinema, independent film, pornography, and their occasional eruptions into mainstream Hollywood and television movies, 'we gain something and we lose something', according to Vito Russo:

> We lose that sense of belonging to a secret world to which no one else has access. What we gain in the specificity of the new cinema – especially independent cinema – is the reality that fourteen-year-old gay kids in Tulsa will be able to go to the movies and not have the idea that they're the only ones in the world who are gay. A future generation of lesbians and gay men will never know that secret world, and I'm torn between wanting to maintain it and letting it go.[1]

I too share such misgivings about losing a rich, hidden film tradition, as I have yet to see a contemporary film with an overtly lesbian theme which has the erotic power of Marlene Dietrich's performance in *Morocco*. But the history of lesbian representation in the cinema is not simply a movement from subtextual signs and gestures in the 1930s to post-gay liberation 'positive images' in the 1980s, with a stop along the way for malicious stereotypes in the 1950s. The cinema has been and continues to be a contested terrain in which people and groups with often opposing interests have staked their claims.

In the earliest film representations of lesbianism, the cinema did not directly subscribe to then-popular medical models and theories of 'female inversion'. The influence of women directors (such as Leontine Sagan and Dorothy Arzner), the intervention of early female stars (such as Louise Brooks and Greta Garbo), and the longings of lesbian spectators combined to revise and redefine these theories in a way that focused on female pleasures rather than perversions. The rise of the Hollywood star system inadvertently created powerful stars who were role models for a lesbian subculture in the process of self-definition. And the magical qualities of the movies themselves, with their insistence on ever-changing theatrical roles, helped legitimize a way of life to which role-playing and masquerade were central experiences.

Even the more direct references to homosexuality which appeared in the 1950s and 60s in the form of stereotypes left room for lesbian spectators to read more satisfying meanings from them, no longer through the ambiguity they offered but now through the contradictions they embodied. For example, the 'butch' or 'mannish lesbian' stereotype of the 1960s could be reworked in the lesbian imagination where 'butch' and 'femme' were means of structuring desire that lacked associations with deviance.

More recently, non-stereotyped images of lesbians have not necessarily meant either ideological improvements or better films, as the frequent appearance of the 'feminine' lesbian vampire suggests. The 1970s and 80s women's and gay liberation movements can be seen to have had a positive impact on the dominant cinema, through the appearance of 'attractive' lesbian characters in such films as *Silkwood* or *Personal Best*, but a closer look at these films reveals that their lesbian relationships are still mapped onto, and seen as poor imitations of, non-lesbian models: mother/daughter has merely replaced male/female. Such films suggest that the lesbian community's ability to appropriate images from the dominant culture is matched or surpassed by the dominant culture's amazing capacity to absorb and co-opt marginalized groups.

Throughout the twentieth century – throughout the period in which the modern concept of 'lesbian identity' has existed – the cinema has been one of the most pervasive cultural influences. Even in its slow decline, it continues to reach vast numbers of people and strongly define the ways in which we live. It must not be seen only as an oppressive institution which instills patriarchal values; nor should it be seen purely as entertainment, without paying attention to the ideological processes at work. The cinema has been in many ways hostile to lesbians, and yet lesbians continue to flock to it.

And more than that, lesbians look to it for ideas about who we are. We have come of age together, and our relationship has a history that can't be dismissed. As the world enters the twenty-first century, the technologies of video, cable television, laser disk, and media not yet invented are already threatening to take the cinema's place. With its demise, perhaps we will feel nostalgia, as Queen Christina did, for something we have never seen: in our case, for a representation of lesbianism that has been all but representable in the cinema.

Notes

INTRODUCTION: THE COLOR VIOLET

1 The importance of the color violet for lesbians is discussed more fully in Judy Grahn, *Another Mother Tongue* (Boston: Beacon Press, 1984), p. 8. Marlene Dietrich's comment about Berlin lesbians is cited in a photo caption in B. Ruby Rich, 'From Repressive Tolerance to Erotic Liberation', *Jump Cut*, 24/25 (March 1981), p. 49. Original source unknown.

2 Patrice Petro, *Joyless Streets: Women and Melodramatic Representation in Weimar Germany*, (N.J.: Princeton University Press, 1989), p. 223.

3 Leila J. Rupp explores the lives of some of these women in her essay ' "Imagine My Surprise": Women's Relationships in Mid-Twentieth Century America', in Martin B. Duberman, Martha Vicinus and George Chauncey, Jr. (eds), *Hidden From History: Reclaiming the Gay and Lesbian Past* (New York: New American Library, 1989).

4 Jeanne Flash Gray, 'Memories', *The Other Black Woman* (1982). Published by the Committee for the Visibility of the Other Black Woman, on file at the Lesbian Herstory Archives.

5 The major works on camp and the gay male subculture are: Susan Sontag, 'Notes on Camp', in *Against Interpretation* (New York: Farrar, Strauss and Giroux, 1966); Michael Bronski, *Cultural Clash: The Making of Gay Sensibility* (Boston: South End Press, 1984); and Jack Babuscio, 'Camp and the Gay Sensibility', in Richard Dyer (ed.), *Gays and Film* (New York: Zoetrope, 1984). One interesting study which considers the importance of camp in lesbian theater is Sue Ellen Case, 'Toward a Butch-Femme Aesthetic', in Lynda Hart (ed.), *Making a Spectacle: Feminist Essays on Contemporary Women's Theater* (Ann Arbor: University of Michigan Press, 1989).

6 John Caughie, 'Playing at being American: Games and Tactics' in Patricia Mellencamp (ed.), *Logics of Television: Essays in Cultural Criticism* (Bloomington: Indiana University Press, 1990).

1 FEMALE PLEASURES AND PERVERSIONS IN THE SILENT AND EARLY SOUND CINEMA

1 This twenty-year period between 1890 and 1910 has been considered by some historians as something of a watershed in the area of sexual theory, out of which the modern concepts of homosexuality and lesbianism were formed. In this time the 'science' of sexology emerged and gained legitimacy, benefiting from the strengthening in status and authority of the medical profession, to which sexology attached

itself. As science asserted the pleasures of order and regulation, sexology stepped in to evaluate, regulate, control and construct new categories of sexual identity. In the process, a new conceptual alignment came into being: a line was now drawn between normal and natural sexuality on the one hand, deviant and unnatural on the other. Where previous distinctions between reproductive or non-reproductive sex placed emphasis on the sex act itself, normal or deviant came to describe the identity of the individual engaging in the act. Focusing on the male homosexual, Michel Foucault succinctly described this shift, 'The sodomite had been a temporary aberration; the homosexual was now a species.' (*The History of Sex*, vol. 1)

A number of feminist historians, including Smith-Rosenberg, have argued that the sexologists, and especially Havelock Ellis, were responsible for shattering the nineteenth-century Victorian homosocial female world by pathologizing women's romantic friendships. Other historians such as John D'Emilio and Estelle Freedman disagree about the importance of the sexologists, claiming that they 'were responding to real changes in the social organization of same sex eroticism'. But whether or not the sexologists created or merely responded to social phenomena, or whether they actually closed down or perhaps unwittingly opened up the possibilities for female sexual and emotional experience at the end of the nineteenth century, through their medical definitions sexologists did describe and popularize, if not create, the modern homosexual and lesbian. Their social categorization, aimed at regulation and control, contributed to the development of what we now consider homosexual identity.

On the role of Havelock Ellis in pathologizing women's friendships, see Carroll Smith-Rosenberg, 'The New Woman as Androgyne: Social Disorder and Gender Crisis, 1870–1936', in *Disorderly Conduct* (New York: Oxford University Press, 1985), p. 267. For a more functional view, see John D'Emilio and Estelle Freedman, *Intimate Matters* (New York: Harper and Row, 1988), p. 226.

2 Havelock Ellis, Appendix B, 'The School-Friendships of Girls', *Studies in the Psychology of Sex*, vol. 2 (New York: Random House, 1936), p. 374.

3 R.W. Shufeldt, 'Dr. Havelock Ellis on Sexual Inversion', *Pacific Medical Journal* XLV (1902), pp. 199–207, cited in Smith-Rosenberg p. 280.

4 Much as during the 'lavender menace' scare of the early 1970s, feminists joined their homophobic attackers rather than be discredited by them. One feminist publication ran a series of essays, entitled 'Spinsters in the Making: the College Woman', warning against female colleges and the pathological attachments they encouraged between women. See 'Spinsters in the Making. Type 1 – The College Woman', the *Freewoman* (28 December, 1911), p. 66.

5 Louise Brooks, *Lulu in Hollywood* (NY: Alfred A. Knopf, 1982), p. 97.

6 B. Ruby Rich, 'From Repressive Tolerance to Erotic Liberation', *Jump Cut*, 24/25 (March 1981), p. 44.

7 Rich, 'Repressive Tolerance', p. 44.

8 Ibid. p. 45.

9 Ibid. p. 46.

10 Vito Russo, *The Celluloid Closet* (New York: Harper and Row, 1981), p. 58.

11 '*Mädchen in Uniform*', *Close-Up*, 10.2 (1933).

12 Smith-Rosenberg, 'New Woman as Androgyne', p. 282.

13 Censorship letters from the Hays Office, housed in the Academy of Motion Picture Arts and Sciences archive, quoted in Russo, *Celluloid Closet*, p. 59.

14 '*Club de Femmes*', *Vice Versa*, 1.2 (April 1947) on file at the Lesbian Herstory Archives, NYC.

15 'Letters', *Vice Versa*, 1.3 (August 1947) on file at the Lesbian Herstory Archives, NYC.

16 Robert Aldrich interview, quoted in Russo, *Celluloid Closet*, p. 50.

17 Program notes on file with Museum of Modern Art Film Library (no date).
18 George Chauncey, 'Christian Brotherhood or Sexual Perversion? Homosexual Identities and the Construction of Sexual Boundaries in the World War I Era', Martin B. Duberman, et al. (eds), *Hidden from History*, p. 546n.
19 Arguments between 'Uranians' and sexologists in the 1910s are explored further in Andrea Weiss, 'On Spinsters, Uranians, and Sexual Inversion: Debates on Sex and Sexology in the *Freewoman*' (June 1989), unpublished paper.
20 Frances Wilder to Edward Carpenter, quoted in Ruth Claus, 'Confronting Homosexuality', *Signs*, II (1977), pp. 928–33.
21 *Close Up* featured the writings of such prominent Modernist female writers as H.D. (Hilda Doolittle), Bryher, Marianne Moore, Dorothy Richardson, and Gertrude Stein, all of whom besides Stein had written for the *Freewoman* in their younger days and must have been well aware of the debates on sexuality in its pages.
22 Smith-Rosenberg, 'New Woman as Androgyne', p. 288.
23 Richard Dyer, 'White', *Screen*, 29.4 (Autumn 1988), pp. 44–64.
24 Esther Newton has proposed as much when she claims that Radclyffe Hall and her circle of friends in England embraced some sexologic definitions as a way of acknowledging their sexual desire. Esther Newton, 'The Mythic Mannish Lesbian: Radclyffe Hall and the New Woman', *Signs* (Summer 1984), pp. 557–75.
   For further information about the visits of Bryher and H.D. to Dr. Havelock Ellis, see the letter from H.D. to Bryher, 14 February 1919, and from Bryher to H.D., 20 March 1919, both in the Beinecke Library, Yale University.
25 Smith-Rosenberg, 'New Woman as Androgyne', p. 282.
26 Brooks, *Lulu in Hollywood*, p. 99.
27 Ibid.
28 Russo, *Celluloid Closet*, p. 25.
29 Louise Brooks, letter to Kevin Brownlow, 29 April 1969, cited in Barry Paris, *Louise Brooks* (NY: Alfred A. Knopf, 1989), p. 416.
30 Quoted in Louise Brooks's letter to Kevin Brownlow, 11 June 1969, in Paris, *Louise Brooks*, p. 239.
31 Louise Brooks, letter to Kevin Brownlow, 29 April 1969. Quoted in Paris, *Louise Brooks*, p. 416.
32 Quoted in Louise Brooks's letter to Kevin Brownlow, 19 October 1968 and in Paris, *Louise Brooks*, p. 239.
33 Louise Brooks, letter to James Card, 29 October 1955, quoted in Paris, *Louise Brooks*, p. 419.
34 Elizabeth B. Hurlock, *The Psychology of Dress: An Analysis of Fashion and its Motive* (New York, 1929), pp. 115–16.
35 Herbert Blumer, *Movies and Conduct* (New York: MacMillan Co., 1933).
36 Ibid. p. 109.
37 Ibid. p. 45.
38 Ibid. p. 71.
39 Henry James Forman, *Our Movie Mad Children* (New York: Macmillan Co., 1933), p. 219.
40 Blumer, *Movies and Conduct*, pp. 70–1.
41 Bryher, 'Defence of Hollywood', *Close-Up*, 2.3 (February 1928).
42 Jane Gaines, 'White Privilege and Looking Relations: Race and Gender in Feminist Film Theory', *Screen*, 29.4 (Autumn 1988), pp. 24–35.

2 'A QUEER FEELING WHEN I LOOK AT YOU': HOLLYWOOD STARS AND LESBIAN SPECTATORSHIP IN THE 1930S

1 Kenneth G. McLain, 'The Untold Story of Marlene Dietrich', *Confidential*, 3 (July 1955), p. 22.

2 Edith Becker, Michelle Citron, Julia Lesage, and B. Ruby Rich, 'Introduction, Lesbians and Film Special Section', *Jump Cut*, 24/25 (March 1981), p. 18.

3 Patricia Meyer Spacks, *Gossip* (New York: Alfred A. Knopf, 1985), p. 46.

4 Andrew Britton, *Katharine Hepburn: The Thirties and After*, (Newcastle upon Tyne: Tyneside Cinema, 1984), p. 16.

5 Cited in the *Morocco* program notes of the D.W. Griffith Film Center, 13 May 1976 screening.

6 Russo, *Celluloid Closet*, p. 14.

7 Homer Dickens, *The Films of Marlene Dietrich* (Secaucus, NJ: The Citadel Press, 1980), p. 19.

8 Becker, et al., 'Introduction, Lesbians and Film', p. 18.

9 Richard Dyer, *Heavenly Bodies: Film Stars and Society* (New York: St. Martins Press, 1986), p. 5.

10 Antony James, 'Remembering the Thirties', *The Yellow Book*, p. 7. On file at the Lesbian Herstory Archives, New York City.

11 This experience of living a 'double life' in the 1930s was a common theme expressed in a series of interviews conducted by the Before Stonewall Film Project, on file at the Lesbian Herstory Archives, New York City.

12 Richard Dyer, *Gays and Film*, p. 1.

13 Russo, *Celluloid Closet*, p. 65.

14 Rebecca Louise Bell-Metereau, *Hollywood Androgyny* (New York: Columbia University Press, 1985), p. 74.

15 H.D., 'The Cinema and the Classics', *Close-Up*, 1 (July 1927).

16 Salka Viertal, *The Kindness of Strangers* (NY: Holt, Rinehart and Winston, 1969), p. 175.

17 Britton, *Katharine Hepburn*, p. 11.

18 Carroll Smith-Rosenberg, 'New Woman as Androgyne', p. 267.

19 Mary Anne Doane, 'Film and the Masquerade: Theorizing the Female Spectator', *Screen*, 23.3–4 (September/October 1982), p. 78.

20 Ibid.

21 Quoted in Judy Whitaker, 'Hollywood Transformed', *Jump Cut*, 24/25 (March 1981), p. 35.

22 Andrea Weiss, unpublished interviews with (Ms.) Christopher Sitwell and Karl Bissinger, on gay life in the 1930s, (May 1988).

23 Lisa Ben, 'Club de Femmes', *Vice Versa*, 1.3 (August 1947), p. 9.

24 Flavia Rando, 'Romaine Brooks: The Creation of a Lesbian Image'. Unpublished paper.

25 The prevalence of 'looking for clues to the self' in medical texts on homosexuality in the 1930s can be seen in interviews conducted by the Before Stonewall Film Project, housed at the Lesbian Herstory Archives.

26 Katharine B. Davis, *Factors in the Sex Life of Twenty-Two Hundred Women* (1929), pp. 290–2.

27 Vern Bullough and Bonnie Bullough, 'Lesbianism in the 1920s and 1930s: A Newfound Study', *Signs*, 2.4 (Summer 1977), pp. 903–4.

28 Smith-Rosenberg, 'New Woman as Androgyne', p. 282.

29 Ibid.

30 *New York Sun* quoted in James Spada, *Hepburn* (Garden City, NY: Doubleday and Co., 1984), p. 57.

31 Smith-Rosenberg, 'New Woman as Androgyne', p. 291.

32 Ibid.

33 E. Ann Kaplan, 'Is the Gaze Male?' in Ann Snitow, Christine Stansell, and Sharon Thompson (eds), *Powers of Desire: The Politics of Sexuality* (New York: Monthly Review Press, 1983), p. 314.

34 Russo, *Celluloid Closet*, p. 66.

3 POST-WAR HOLLYWOOD LESBIANS: WHOSE HAPPY ENDING?

1 The term 'sex/gender system' was first used by Gayle Rubin in her influential essay, 'The Traffic in Women: Notes on the "Political Economy" of Sex', in Rayna R. Reiter (ed.), *Toward an Anthropology of Women* (New York: Monthly Review Press, 1975), pp. 157–210.

2 This joke is recounted in Lillian Faderman, '*The Children's Hour* in Fact and Fiction: Changing Perspectives on a Lesbian Theme', paper presented at the UCLA gay and lesbian media conference, January 1983.

3 Jackie Stacey discusses this dynamic in *All About Eve* in her essay, 'Desperately Seeking Difference', *Screen*, 28.1 (Winter 1987).

4 Richard Dyer points out these functions in his 'Homosexuality and Film Noir', *Jump Cut*, 16 (November 1977).

5 Ibid.

6 Some of this correspondence has been published in Gerald Gardner, *The Censorship Papers* (NY: Dodd Mead and Co., 1987).

7 Censorship files on *Rebecca* at the Academy of Motion Picture Arts and Sciences, Los Angeles.

8 See Allen Berube, *Coming Out Under Fire: Lesbian and Gay Americans and the Military During World War II* (New York: Free Press, 1989).

9 Madeline Davis and Elizabeth Lapovsky Kennedy, 'Oral History and the Study of Sexuality in the Lesbian Community: Buffalo, New York, 1940–1960', in Martin B. Duberman, et al. (eds), *Hidden From History*, pp. 426–40.

10 Edmund Bergler, M.D., *One Thousand Homosexuals* (Paterson: N.J.: Pageant Books, 1959), p. ix. The list of medical definitions is from Susan Krieger, 'Lesbian Identity and Community: Recent Social Science Literature', *Signs* (Autumn 1982), p. 93.

11 Sigmund Freud, *Three Essays in the Theory of Sexuality* (New York: Basic Books, 1962), p. 95.

12 Sander Gilman, 'Black Bodies, White Bodies: Toward an Iconography of Female Sexuality in Late 19th Century Art, Medicine, and Literature', in Henry Louis Gates, Jr. (ed.), '*Race,' Writing, and Difference* (Chicago: University of Chicago Press, 1985), p. 206).

13 Censorship files on *Children of Loneliness* at the New York State Education Department Archive, Division of Motion Pictures.

14 Edwin Schur, *Labeling Women Deviant: Gender, Stigma, and Social Control* (NY: Random House, 1984), pp. 8–9.

15 Richard Kwietniowsky, 'Meet Cute', *Love Stories* (Exeter, Great Britain: South West Arts, 1983).

16 Caroline Sheldon, 'Lesbians and Film: Some Thoughts', in Richard Dyer (ed.), *Gays and Film*, pp. 5–26.

17 Vito Russo, *Celluloid Closet*.

18 Dyer, 'Stereotyping', in *Gays and Film*, pp. 27, 30.

19 Simon Watney, 'Hollywood's Homosexual World', *Screen*, 23.3–4 (September/October 1982), p. 108.

20 Andrea Weiss, 'From the Margins: New Images of Gays in the Cinema', *Cineaste*, 15.1 (1986), pp. 4–8.

21 Dyer, 'Stereotyping', p. 32.

22 Annette Kuhn, *Women's Pictures*, p. 86.

23 Dyer, 'Stereotyping', p. 30.
24 Sheldon, 'Lesbians and Film', p. 16.
25 Gene Damon, *The Ladder* (February/March 1969), pp. 44–5.
26 The lesbian bar culture of the 1960s is explored in the documentary film *Before Stonewall* and the transcripts of interviews from this film project, conducted by myself and others, are on file at the Lesbian Herstory Archive in New York City. An insight-ful study of the lesbian bar culture before the sixties is Davis and Kennedy, 'Oral History', pp. 426–40. Sue Ellen Case criticizes the assimilationist goals of *Daughters of Bilitis* in her essay, 'Toward a Butch-Femme Aesthetic', in Lynda Hart (ed.), *Making a Spectacle: Feminist Essays on Contemporary Women's Theater* (Ann Arbor: University of Michigan Press, 1989).
27 Kwietniowsky, 'Meet Cute'.
28 Diane Hamer, ' "I Am a Woman": Ann Bannon and the Writing of Lesbian Identity in the 1950s', *Lesbian and Gay Writing*, p. 69.
29 'That Kind of Love', *Time* (9 February 1962), p. 83. Additional miscellaneous reviews and synopsis of *The Children's Hour* on file at the Museum of Modern Art Film Library.
30 Faderman, '*The Children's Hour*', p. 15.
31 Quote from William Wyler on file at the Museum of Modern Art Film Library.
32 Gardner, *The Censorship Papers*.
33 Russo, *Celluloid Closet*, p. 158.
34 John Clum, ' "Something Cloudy, Something Clear": Homophobic Discourse in Tennessee Williams', *South Atlantic Quarterly*, 88.1 (Winter 1989), p. 162.
35 Ibid. p. 165.
36 T.J. Jackson Lears, 'From Salvation to Self-Realization: Advertising and the Thera-peutic Roots of Consumer Culture, 1880–1930', Richard Wight Fox and T.J. Jackson Lears (eds), *The Culture of Consumption: Critical Essays in American History, 1880–1980* (New York: Pantheon Books, 1983), p. 5.
37 Linda Williams, '*Personal Best*: Women in Love', in Charlotte Brunsdon (ed.), *Film for Women* (London: British Film Institute, 1986), pp. 146–54.
38 Elizabeth Ellsworth, 'Illicit Pleasures: Feminist Spectators and *Personal Best*', *Wide Angle*, 8.2 (1986), pp. 45–56.
39 Ibid. p. 47.
40 Williams, '*Personal Best*', p. 149.
41 Robert Towne, *Soho News*, (16 February 1982).
42 Andrew Sarris, *Village Voice*, (26 December 1968), p. 45.
43 Ellsworth, 'Illicit Pleasures', p. 52.
44 Ibid. p. 53.
45 Chris Straayer, '*Personal Best*: Lesbian/ Feminist Audience', *Jump Cut*, 29 (1984), pp. 40–4.
46 An examination of Hollywood 'female friendship' films of the 1970s and early 80s which use lesbianism as an unacceptable boundary can be found in Claudette Charbonneau and Lucy Winer, 'Lesbians in "Nice" Films', *Jump Cut*, 24/25 (March 1981), pp. 25–6.
47 Williams, '*Personal Best*', p. 151.
48 For a theoretical essay on black women's responses to the film *The Color Purple*, see Jacqueline Bobo, 'The Color Purple: Black Women as Cultural Readers', E. Diedre Pribram (ed.), *Female Spectators: Looking at Film and Television* (New York: Verson, 1988). Bobo argues that black women who feel strongly attached to the film have an oppositional response to it; that is, they can appreciate the film while remaining opposed to 'the system that produced [it]'.
49 Molly Hite, 'Writing – And Reading – the Body: Female Sexuality and Recent Feminist Fiction', *Feminist Studies*, 14.1 (Spring 1988), 141n.

50 Michele Wallace, 'Blues For Mr. Spielberg', *Village Voice*, (18 March 1986), p. 24.

4 THE VAMPIRE LOVERS

1 Bertha Harris, 'What is a Lesbian?' *Sinister Wisdom*, 3 (1977).
2 Richard Dyer, 'It's In Their Kiss: Vampirism as Homosexuality, Homosexuality as Vampirism', unpublished paper, 5.
3 Susan Sontag, 'Persona', *Sight and Sound*, 36.4 (Autumn 1967), pp. 186, 191.
4 Lillian Faderman, *Surpassing the Love of Men* (New York: William Morrow and Co., 1981), pp. 341–6.
5 Gene Damon, *The Ladder* (February/March 1971), p. 36; (June/July 1971), pp. 47–8.
6 Conversation with Tudor Gates, screen-writer of the Hammer lesbian vampire trilogy, on 16 January 1992, London.
7 Bonnie Zimmerman, 'Daughters of Darkness: Lesbian Vampires', *Jump Cut*, 24/25 (Fall 1980), p. 23.
8 James Donald, 'The Fantastic, the Sublime and the Popular, or What's At Stake in Vampire Films?', James Donald (ed.), *Fantasy and the Cinema* (London: British Film Institute, 1989), p. 237.
9 Christopher Craft, ' "Kiss Me with Those Ruby Lips": Gender and Inversion in Bram Stoker's *Dracula*', *Representations*, 8 (Fall 1984), p. 109.
10 This fascination with the genitals of female 'inverts' in the turn of the century is discussed in George Chauncey, Jr., 'From Sexual Inversion to Homosexuality: Medicine and the Changing Conceptualization of Female Deviance', *Salmagundi*, 58–59 (1982), pp. 114–46.
11 Craft, 'Kiss Me', p. 109.
12 Linda Williams, 'When the Woman Looks', Mary Ann Doane, Patricia Mellencamp, and Linda Williams (eds), *Revision: Feminist Essays in Film Analysis* (Washington, D.C.: American Film Institute, 1984), p. 87.
13 Conversation with Tudor Gates, screenwriter, on 16 January 1992, London.
14 Theda Bara, interviewed in *Theatre Magazine* (June 1917), p. 246, cited in Lary May, *Screening Out the Past: The Birth of Mass Culture and the Motion Picture Industry* (New York: Oxford University Press, 1980).
15 This 'body double' rumor was first brought to my attention by the writer Michelle Cliff, in conversation in July 1991.
16 The life and legends of Elisabeth Bathory are discussed in Raymond T. McNally, *Dracula Was a Woman* (New York: McGraw Hill, 1983) and David Pirie, *The Vampire Cinema* (Quanto, 1977).
17 Raymond Bellour, 'psychosis, neurosis, perversion', *Camera Obscura*, 3/4 (1979), p. 121.
18 Williams, 'When the Woman Looks', p. 97.
19 Donald, 'The Fantastic, Sublime and the Popular', p. 247.
20 Zimmerman, 'Daughters of Darkness', p. 24.
21 Sontag, 'Notes on Camp'.
22 Babuscio, 'Camp and the Gay Sensibility', p. 43.
23 Ibid. p. 48.
24 Sontag, 'Notes on Camp', p. 275.
25 At the early 1970s Film Series organized by Vito Russo at the Gay Liberation 'Firehouse' in New York City, recounted by Arnie Kantrowitz on the occasion of Vito Russo's memorial service, November 1990.

5 WOMEN'S 'ART' CINEMA AND THE LESBIAN POTENTIAL

1 An example of an art-house film that was extremely problematic for lesbian spectators was Fassbinder's *Bitter Tears of Petra von Kant* which was picketed by New York's Lesbian Feminist Liberation on its release in 1972. For Fassbinder see the chapter on *The Bitter Tears of Petra von Kant* in Timothy Corrigan, *New German Film: The*

Displaced Image, and on Bergman the section on *Persona* in Frank Gado, *The Passion of Ingmar Bergman*.

2   This chapter focuses on European cinema, specifically films from Belgium, the Netherlands, West Germany, and France, each of which has its own distinct film history and culture, although there are commonalities to be found. The European art cinema practice, however, has also extended to work produced in North America and Britain. These film categories do not have rigid formal or national boundaries.

3   Richard Dyer, *Now You See It* (New York: Routledge, 1990), p. 272.

4   Charlotte Brunsdon, (ed.), *Film for Women* (London: BFI, 1986), p. 56.

5   David Bordwell, 'Art Cinema as a Mode of Film Practise', *Film Criticism*, 4.1 (Fall 1979), p. 56.

6   Ibid. p. 58.

7   Brunsdon, *Film for Women*, p. 55.

8   These pronouns can be found on the English-subtitled print of the film; the recent video release seems to have eliminated the relevant subtitles altogether.

9   Amy Taubin, 'I is Another', *Village Voice*, (31 December 1985), p. 70.

10 Ibid. p. 70.

11 Janet Maslin, 'Je Tu Il Elle', *New York Times*, (27 December 1985), c27.

12 Pamela Pratt, *New York Native*, (19 September 1988).

13 Chantal Akerman quoted in essay by Laura Mulvey on Akerman's films, *Time Out* (25–31 May 1980).

14 Mandy Merck, 'Lianna and the Lesbians of Art Cinema', in Brunsdon, *Film for Women*, p. 166.

15 Bordwell, 'Art Cinema', p. 59.

16 *Les Rendez-Vous D'Anna* was screened at the 'Women's Film: Feminist Readings?' program at the University of London, January 1989, followed by a discussion led by Susannah Radstone in which these feelings were expressed. The film was also screened at the Collective for Living Cinema in New York City in 1983 and at the New York Lesbian and Gay Experimental Film Festival in 1989, and a number of lesbian friends articulated these feelings in informal discussions after the screenings.

17 Richard Kwietniowsky, 'Meet Cute', in *Love Stories* (Exeter: Southwest Arts, 1983).

18 Jeanette Murphy raises this point in her essay, '*A Question of Silence*', in Brunsdon, *Film for Women*, p. 107.

19 Brunsdon, *Film for Women*, p. 57.

20 Janet Maslin, *New York Times* (18 March 1983).

21 Ruby Rich, *Village Voice* (17 August 1984).

22 Quotes are from, in this order, Janet Maslin, *New York Times* (18 March 1983); Stanley Kaufman, the *New Republic* (3 September 1984); Archer Winston, *New York Post* (6 August 1984); Philip French, the *Observer*, London, (20 February 1983).

23 Andrea Weiss, 'Refusing to be a Victim: An Interview with Marlene Gorris', *New York Native* (25 March 1985), p. 27.

24 Murphy, '*A Question of Silence*', p. 100.

25 Jill Godmillow, quoted in program notes for the London Gay and Lesbian Film Festival at the National Film Theatre, London, October/November 1988, p. 9.

26 Jill Godmillow and Mark Magill, 'A Page for the Literal Minded: An Account of What in *Waiting for the Moon* is Fact, and What is Just Plain Poetic License', in Skouras Pictures' press kit for *Waiting for the Moon*, 1987.

27 Jane Root, 'Distributing *A Question of Silence*: A Cautionary Tale', in Brunsdon, *Film for Women*, p. 217.

28 Merck, 'Lianna and the Lesbians of Art Cinema', p. 173.

29 Mary Alemany-Galway, 'Lea Pool's *Anne Trister*', *Cinema Canada* (April 1986), p. 22.

30 Ibid.

31 Thomas Elsaesser writes that Ottinger's work creates 'ambivalent spectator per-

spectives, refusing unambiguous strategies of identification', in *Elsaesser, New German Cinema: A History* (New Brunswick: Rutgers University Press, 1989), p. 199.

32 In addition to having a relationship to these more marginal film practices, Ottinger's work has also been seen by some as a feminist revision of classic Hollywood film. For example, Patricia White considers *Madame X* as a remake of the Hollywood melodrama of the same name, in Patricia White, 'Madame X of the China Seas: A Study of Ulrike Ottinger's Film', *Screen*, 28.4 (Autumn 1987), p. 84.

33 Brunsdon, *Film for Women*, pp. 55–6.

34 This use of the 'double' is frequently found in Ottinger's work, such as in her use of Siamese twins in *Freak Orlando* (1981) and in the creation of a second Dorian Gray, a narcissistic projection in *Dorian Gray in the Reflection of the Yellow Press* (1984).

35 Teresa de Lauretis, *Technologies of Gender: Essays on Theory, Film and Fiction* (Bloomington: University of Indiana Press, 1987), p. 131.

36 The importance of the character of Bellcampo in the film's address to marginal spectators is discussed by White, *'Madame X'*, pp. 91–2.

37 Marc Silberman, 'Surreal Images: Interview with Ulrike Ottinger', *Jump Cut*, 29 (1984), p. 56.

38 Claudia Lenssen, in Helen Fehervary, Claudia Lenssen, and Judith Mayne, 'From Hitler to Hepburn: A Discussion of Women's Film Production and Reception', *New German Critique*, 24–25 (Fall/Winter 1981–82), p. 184.

39 White, *'Madame X'*, p. 80.

6 TRANSGRESSIVE CINEMA: LESBIAN INDEPENDENT FILM

1 'Iris Films Fundraising for Lesbian Mothers Film', *Lesbian Tide*, 5.4 (March/April 1976), p. 8.

2 One of many such announcements appears in *Lesbian Tide*, 5.4 (March/April 1976), p. 8.

3 Alice Bloch, 'An Interview with Jan Oxenberg', *Amazon Quarterly*, 2.2 (December 1973), p. 54.

4 Radicalesbians, 'Woman-Identified-Woman' (1970), reprinted in Karla Jay and Allen Young (eds) *Out of the Closets* (New York: Jove/HBJ Books, 1977).

5 Ibid. p. 176.

6 Brooke, 'The Retreat to Cultural Feminism', in Redstockings, *Feminist Revolution* (New York: Random House, 1978).

7 Michelle Citron, 'Comic Critique: Films of Jan Oxenberg', *Jump Cut*, 24/25 (1981), p. 31.

8 Richard Dyer uses Barbara Hammer's films to define this cultural feminist position. See Dyer, *Now You See It*, pp. 194–206.

9 Barbara Hammer, quoted in Jacqueline Zita, 'Counter-Currencies of a Lesbian Iconography: Films of Barbara Hammer', *Jump Cut*, 24/25 (1981), p. 29.

10 Ibid. p. 28.

11 For a fairly complete listing of these early lesbian films with brief descriptions, see Andrea Weiss, 'Filmography of Lesbian Works', *Jump Cut*, 24/25 (1981) pp. 22, 50–1.

12 Zita, 'Counter-Currencies of a Lesbian Iconography', p. 28.

13 Dot Tuer, 'Pleasure in the Dark: Sexual Difference and Erotic Deviance in the Articulation of a Female Desire', *CineAction!* (Fall 1987), p. 56.

14 Monique Wittig, *Les Guerillères* (New York: Viking Press, 1971).

15 Andrea Weiss, 'Becoming Visible: On Doing Research in Lesbian and Gay History' in Andrea Weiss and Greta Schiller, *Before Stonewall: The Making of a Gay and Lesbian Community* (Tallahassee, Fl: Naiad Press, 1988), p. 72.

16 Monica Dorenkamp, 'Hell Divin'' *Outweek* (16 May 1990), p. 65.

17 Helen Fehervary, et al., 'From Hitler to Hepburn', p. 176.

18 This black gay male aesthetic, it could be argued, in part relies upon the aesthetic of white gay male artists such as Carl Van Vechten and George Platt Lynes in the

1930s, Robert Mapplethorpe in the 70s, toward black gay male images.

19 For more on the myth of black matriarchy, see Angela Y. Davis, *Women, Race and Class* (New York: Random House, 1981).

20 Sheila McLaughlin in 'She Must Be Seeing Things: An Interview with Sheila McLaughlin by Alison Butler', *Screen*, 28.4 (Autumn 1987), pp. 21–22.

21 Teresa de Lauretis, 'Technologies of Gender', p. 141.

22 For two excellent works on the meaning of the butch/femme relationship in the lesbian subculture, see Joan Nestle, 'Butch-Fem Relationships, Sexual Courage in the 1950s', *Heresies* 12 (1981), pp. 21–4, and Judy Grahn, *Another Mother Tongue: Gay Words, Gay Worlds* (Boston: Beacon Press, 1984).

23 Martha Gever, 'Girl Crazy: Lesbian Narratives in *She Must Be Seeing Things* and *Damned If You Don't*', the *Independent* (July 1988), p. 17.

24 McLaughlin, 'She Must Be Seeing Things', p. 22.

25 Barbara Hammer, 'Does Radical Content Require Radical Form?' *Millennium Film Journal*, 22 (Winter/Spring 1989–90).

26 Claudia Gorbman, 'Body Displaced, Body Discovered: Recent Work of Barbara Hammer', *Jump Cut*, 32 (April 1986), p. 12.

27 Ibid.

AFTERWORD:

1 Vito Russo, Gay Studies Conference, Yale University, 1987.

Selected Filmography

Distribution information for the United States and United Kingdom follows those titles which are not widely available on home video. A more extensive lesbian filmography is being compiled by Jenni Olsen, c/o Frameline, PO Box 14792, San Francisco CA 94114. Key distribution sources for lesbian films beyond those listed here are Frameline, Women Make Movies (225 Lafayette St., New York NY 10012), and Cinemien (Entrepotdek 66, Amsterdam 1018 AD, The Netherlands).

Anne Trister, dir. Lea Pool
Films Vision 4 Inc., Canada
1985 35mm fiction color
Telefilm Canada, Tour de la Banque Nationale,
600 rue La Janchetiere W., 14th fl., Montreal, Quebec H3B 4L2

Before Stonewall: The Making of a Gay and Lesbian Community, dir. Greta Schiller
Before Stonewall, Inc., United States
1985 16mm documentary color
Cinema Guild, 1697 Broadway, New York, NY 10019
Jane Balfour Films Ltd, 35 Fortess Rd, London NW5 2AD
home video: Naiad Press, PO Box 10543, Tallahassee, FL 32302

Blonde Venus, dir. Josef von Sternberg
Paramount Pictures, United States
1932 35mm fiction b/w

Blood and Roses (Et Mourir de Plaisir), dir. Roger Vadim
Documento, France/Italy
1960 35mm fiction color
Paramount Nontheatrical, 5451 Marathon Street, Hollywood, CA 90038
United Int'l Pictures, Mortimer House, 37–41 Mortimer Street, London W1A 2JL

Borderline, dir. Kenneth MacPherson
The Pool Group, England
1930 16mm experimental narrative b/w silent
Museum of Modern Art, 11 West 53rd Street, New York, NY 10019
British Film Institute, 21 Stephen Street, London W1P 1PL

Born in Flames, dir. Lizzie Borden
United States
1983 16mm fiction color
First Run Features, 153 Waverly Place, New York, NY 10014
Cine Nova, 113 Roman Road, London E2 0HU
home video: First Run Features

The Children's Hour (U.K. title: *The Loudest Whisper*),
Mirisch, United States, dir. William Wyler
1961 35mm fiction b/w
Swank Films, 350 Vanderbilt Motor Pkwy, Hauppauge, NY 11787
United Int'l Pictures, Mortimer House, 37–41 Mortimer Street, London W1A 2JL

Club de Femmes, dir. Jacques Duval
Ccb Jacques Deval, France
1936 16mm fiction b/w
Em Gee Film Library, 6924 Canby Avenue, suite 103, Reseda, CA 91335
British Film Institute, 21 Stephen Street, London W1P 1PL

The Color Purple, dir. Steven Spielberg
Amblin Entertainment, United States
1985 35mm fiction color

Damned If You Don't, dir. Su Friedrich
United States
1987 16mm experimental b/w
Women Make Movies, Inc., 225 Lafayette Street, New York, NY 10012
London Filmmakers' Cooperative, 42 Gloucester Avenue, London NW1 8JD
home video: Ladyslipper Inc., 613 Vickers Avenue, Durham, NC 27701

Daughters of Darkness (La Rouge aux Lèvres), dir. Harry Kumel
Showking Film, Belgium
1970 35mm fiction color

Dracula's Daughter, dir. Lambert Hillyer
Universal, United States
1936 35mm fiction b/w
Swank Films, 350 Vanderbilt Motor Pkwy, Hauppauge, NY 11787

Entre Nous (Coup de Foudre), dir. Diane Kurys
Partners Production/Alexandre Films, France
1983 35mm fiction color
Orion Pictures, 540 Madison Avenue, New York, NY 10022
Gala Films, 26 Danbury Street, Islington, London N1 8JU

Gently Down the Stream, dir. Su Friedrich
United States
1981 16mm experimental b/w silent
Women Make Movies, Inc., 225 Lafayette Street, New York, NY 10012
London Filmmakers' Cooperative, 42 Gloucester Avenue, London NW1 8JD

Home Movie, dir. Jan Oxenberg
United States
1973 16mm experimental color
Frameline, PO Box 14792, San Francisco, CA 94114
Cine Nova, 113 Roman Road, London E2 0HU

The Hunger, dir. Tony Scott
Richard Shepherd, United States
1980 35mm fiction color

In the Best Interests of the Children, dir. Liz Stevens,
    Frances Reid, and Cathy Zheutlin
Iris Films, United States
1977 16mm documentary color
Women Make Movies, Inc., 225 Lafayette Street, New York, NY 10012

Je Tu Il Elle, dir. Chantal Akerman
Paradise Films, Belgium/France
1974 35mm experimental b/w
World Artists, Inc., PO Box 36788, Los Angeles, CA 90036
Metro Pictures Ltd., 79 Wardour Street, London W1V 3TH
home video: World Artists, Inc.

Joanna D'Arc of Mongolia, dir. Ulrike Ottinger
Ulrike Ottinger Filmproduktion, West Germany
1988 35mm experimental narrative color
Women Make Movies, Inc., 225 Lafayette Street, New York, NY 10012

The Killing of Sister George, dir. Robert Aldrich
Palomar, United States
1968 35mm fiction color

Madame X: An Absolute Ruler (Madame X: Eine Absolute Herscherin),
    dir. Ulrike Ottinger
Autoren Film Ulrike Ottinger/Tabea Blumenschein, West Germany
1977 16mm experimental narrative color
Exportfilm Bischoff, Isabellastr. 20, D-8000 Munich, Germany

Mädchen in Uniform, dir. Leontine Sagan
Deutsche Film-Gemeinschaft, Germany
1931 35mm fiction b/w
Films Inc., 5547 N. Ravenswood Avenue, Chicago, IL 60640–1199
British Film Institute, 21 Stephen Street, London W1P 1PL

Manhattan, dir. Woody Allen
United Artists, United States
1979 35mm fiction b/w

Morocco, dir. Josef von Sternberg
Paramount, United States
1930 35mm fiction b/w

Night of the Iguana, dir. John Huston
Seven Arts, United States
1964 35mm fiction b/w
Swank films, 350 Vanderbilt Motor Pkwy, Hauppauge, NY 11787
Filmbank Dist., Grayton House, 498–504 Fulham Road, London SW6 5NH

Pandora's Box (Die Büchse der Pandora), dir. G.W. Pabst
Nero Film, Germany
1928 35mm fiction b/w silent

Personal Best, dir. Robert Towne
Geffen Co./Warner Bros., United States
1983 35mm fiction color

Queen Christina, dir. Rouben Mamoulian
MGM, United States
1933 35mm fiction b/w
Films Inc., 5547 N. Ravenswood Avenue, Chicago, IL 60640–1199
Filmbank Dist., Grayton House, 498–504 Fulham Road, London SW6 5NH

A Question of Silence (De Stilte Rond Christina M.),
    dir. Marlene Gorris
Sigma Films, The Netherlands
1983 35mm fiction color
Quartet Films, 1414 Avenue of the Americas, New York, NY 10019
Glenbuck Films, Glenbuck Road, Surbiton, Surrey KT6 6BT

Les Rendez-Vous d'Anna, dir. Chantal Akerman
Paradise Films, Belgium/France
1978 35mm experimental narrative b/w
World Artists, Inc., PO Box 36788, Los Angeles, CA 90036
Metro Pictures, Ltd., 79 Wardour Street, London W1V 3TH
home video: World Artists, Inc.

She Must Be Seeing Things, dir. Sheila McLaughlin
United States
1987 16mm fiction color
First Run Features, 153 Waverly Place, New York, NY 10014
Metro Pictures, Ltd., 79 Wardour Street, London W1V 3TH
home video: First Run Features

Silkwood, dir. Mike Nichols
ABC Motion Pictures Production, United States
1983 35mm fiction color

Storme: Lady of the Jewel Box, dir. Michelle Parkerson
Eye of the Storm Productions, United States
1987 16mm documentary color
Women Make Movies, Inc., 225 Lafayette Street, New York, NY 10012
Cine Nova, 113 Roman Road, London E2 0HO

Sylvia Scarlett, dir. George Cukor
RKO, United States
1935 35mm fiction b/w
Films Inc., 5547 N. Ravenswood Avenue, Chicago, IL 60640–1199
Glenbuck Films, Glenbuck Road, Surbiton, Surrey KT6 6BT

Sync Touch, dir. Barbara Hammer
Goddess Films, United States
1981 16mm experimental color
Women Make Movies, Inc., 225 Lafayette Street, New York, NY 10012
home video: Facets Multimedia, 1517 W. Fullerton, Chicago IL 60614

Tiny & Ruby: Hell Divin' Women, dir. Greta Schiller and Andrea Weiss
Jezebel Productions, United States
1988 16mm documentary color
Cinema Guild, 1697 Broadway, New York NY 10019
British Film Institute, 21 Stephen Street, London W1P 1PL
home video: Jezebel Productions, PO Box 1348, New York, NY 10011

The Vampire Lovers, dir. Roy Ward Baker
Hammer Studio, Great Britain
1970 35mm fiction color

Waiting for the Moon, dir. Jill Godmillow
New Front Films, United States
1987 35mm fiction color
Skouras Pictures, 1040 N. Las Palmas Avenue, Hollywood, CA 90038

The Wild Party, dir. Dorothy Arzner
Paramount Pictures, United States
1929 35mm fiction b/w
Swank Films, 350 Vanderbilt Motor Pkwy, Hauppauge, NY 11787

Picture Credits

For photographs other than those in my own collection I am grateful to the following sources:

Lizzie Borden, p.152 top; British Film Institute, pp.15 top, 16, 19, 23 top, 65 bottom, 68, 75, 81, 95 bottom, 99, 100, 102 bottom, 124 top, 127 bottom; Cinémathèque Française, p.23 bottom; FPG International, p.49; Su Friedrich, pp.158, 160; Barbara Hammer, pp.141, 156; Hammer Film Studios, pp.89, 95 top, 97; Kobal Collection, p.25; Metro Pictures, pp.116 bottom, 152 bottom; Ulrike Ottinger, pp.134, 135; Greta Schiller, p.147 top; Skouras Pictures Inc. (© 1987 Skouras Pictures Inc./© 1987 Laboratory for Icon and Idiom Inc.), p.124 bottom; World Artists Inc., p.116 top.

Index